RESURRECTING CHURCH

RESURRECTING CHURCH

Where Justice and Diversity Meet Radical
Welcome and Healing Hope

John Cleghorn

Foreword by
Rodney S. Sadler Jr.

FORTRESS PRESS
MINNEAPOLIS

RESURRECTING CHURCH

Where Justice and Diversity Meet Radical Welcome and Healing Hope

Print ISBN: 978-1-5064-6484-8

eBook ISBN: 978-1-5064-6485-5

Cover design: Laurie Ingram

Cover Art: *Born of Water, Born of Spirit* by Jan Richardson / janrichardson.com

To the Lord, God of grace, mercy and justice, for this calling; to my family, Kelly, Ellison and Sophie, for their understanding; to my parents, for shaping me; and, to my wondrous congregation, for abiding along our journey.

CONTENTS

FOREWORD

It was the first Saturday afternoon in June, the day after the 2020 George Floyd–inspired Uprising began in Charlotte, North Carolina. A group of clergy had been summoned by Charlotte's mayor Vi Lyles and city manager Marcus Jones to help them manage the crisis unfolding before them. In the streets the evening before there had been excessive violence and racial strife; the city was moments away from coming undone. There were about twenty of us clergy gathered in the large multipurpose room of Belmont Community Center on that day. We wore masks and kept social distance as a result of intersecting crises; the Uprisings occurred during the COVID-19 quarantine, making the violence of the prior evening even more troubling. The resonant baritone voice and seasoned Southern drawl of one of the three white male ministers in the room seemed to hold the attention of the city leaders as he talked about what might make for peace and justice in these troubled times. Because of the diversity and unique character of the congregation he pastored, he had a particular credibility with those in city leadership.

After this meeting I found myself in the company of Rev. Veronica Cannon and that man, this book's author, Rev. Dr. John Cleghorn. We'd found our way to a rare open restaurant where we would be able to socially distance as we broke bread together. It was a blessed occasion. I was with two of my dear former students who have both excelled in ministry, and we had a chance to sit together and debrief as we pondered yet another police killing of an unarmed Black man.

As we sat in the open dining room, I noticed that we were just across the street from Covenant Presbyterian Church. This faith community is one of the most influential main-line congregations in the city, comprised of a large member-ship of affluent "white" people who were among the city's most prominent leaders. It was not by mistake that John led us to this restaurant, for it was across the street from his for-mer church home. It was there that he began his ministry over a decade ago, there that I had first heard him preach, and from there that he left to take his first senior pastoral charge at Caldwell Presbyterian Church. This was a restau-rant that he and his family frequented after Sunday worship services while they were Covenant members.

During a lull in the conversation, after staring at Covenant for a time, I asked John if, should the current pas-tor of Covenant ever leave for any reason, he would like to return to his old congregation as senior pastor. After all, Covenant was the church of former Bank of America CEO Hugh McColl (John's former boss when in another life he was a senior vice president at that bank) and many other executives from banking and other industries. Covenant was the site of remarkable work addressing affordable hous-ing in Charlotte, helping create hundreds of economically accessible apartments across the city. Covenant had even made a name for itself as one of the few congregations in the city that was leading dialogue on reconciliation between Israelis and Palestinians. Covenant was the kind of ground-breaking big-steeple church that many waited their entire careers to pastor. Without skipping a beat, he exclaimed a bold and decisive, "No!"

Having known John throughout his ministry, his answer did not surprise me. For he had become identified with the spirit of Caldwell Presbyterian Church, an intentionally intersectional congregation that brought together people white and Black, straight and LGBTQ, wealthy and impoverished, English and Spanish speaking, old and young. It is a vibrant space filled with a diverse cadre of mostly progressive congregants eager to live out God's vision of inclusive welcome in the Elizabeth community of Charlotte. The members had long since become like family to John, for he had guided them through many conflicts and crises as they struggled with the question of whether they would be a mainline congregation that chose to emphasize racial reconciliation, LGBTQ inclusion, bridging the class divide, or welcoming our Latinx siblings, and to all the congregation answered emphatically, "Yes!"

Serving as the senior pastor at Caldwell had not been an easy calling. Indeed, it almost crushed John at different points as the intersecting oppressed communities struggled for attention and primacy, often leaving John to be both pastor and conflict moderator, standing alone between factions, at the cross. But the cross is the essence of intersection, and there Jesus is found, and John, though broken, found wholeness again and again and again, becoming ever more convinced that this was the ministry to which God had called him.

It is from his innovative ministry in that diverse context that this book was born. It is an examination of his journey. It is a roadmap to the land mines along that perilous way, attested by one who had on occasion triggered them. It is a research project that sets the Caldwell experience in the context of the small handful of other similarly situated intersectional congregations. But more than that, it is an invitation for you to reimagine what church can be—no, what it should be—when we are open to the free movement of the Spirit and the transformative power of being "in Christ" (Gal 3:28).

Caldwell Presbyterian Church is a community of people whose story deserves to be told. In a world that is increasingly divided along lines of difference exacerbated by the political realities of retrenched supremacy, nationalism, homophobia, and xenophobia in the aftermath of the 2016 elections, Caldwell is an oasis of convergence replete with many people who would be overlooked and underappreciated outside of the sanctuary's doors. Yet here they are choir members, ushers, ministers, and elders on session; here these people lead a distinctive intentional community that is reflective of Dr. King's ideal of "Beloved Community"; here they are the manifestation of the marginalized multiethnic menagerie who made up the original first-century church in Palestine, Egypt, Ethiopia, and throughout the Greco-Roman Empire. Yes, Caldwell is in many respects radical inasmuch as it reflects the diverse roots of the Christian faith.

And John does more in this text than just tell their story. In a very careful way, he relates their narrative in connection with those of nine other similarly constituted congregations. All of them seem to have been intentionally crafted to be intersectional in response to the impending death of each worshipping community. The browning of the communities where they were located caused a decline in membership of these originally historic "white" congregations. Faced with the inevitability of death if they didn't change, these congregations chose change, significant change,

change unusual in a world where congregations tend to be communities of those celebrating their "sameness." Because of this change, congregational death gave way to new life; death gave way to resurrection!

So, with the great skill of an accomplished storyteller (a journalist in a previous life) and careful analysis of a trained researcher, John explores what makes these congregations work as exemplars for the contemporary church. His engagement with biblical, theological, and congregational scholarship herein is second to none in this regard, yet he retains the ability to share deep insights with a familiar Southern approachability and with the tenor of Georgian vernacular idiom. As a biblical scholar, I would be remiss if I did not note his care to provide a thorough exegetical analysis of Galatians 3:27–28, made all the more significant by his attention to the voices of minoritized communities as they have read this text. As a result, this text will prove useful both to religious academics and pastoral practitioners seeking to understand the intricate open secrets of inter-sectional congregations and to theologically untrained congregants looking for a gripping, hopeful, and theologically moving narrative to fill a quiet afternoon.

To be unabashedly candid, this book is not just a pleasant nod to Rodney King's now famous query, "Can we all just get along?" No, this is a book about justice—justice in all its difficulty, messiness, and patent discomfort. John does more than just exclaim the humanity of his congregants whose identities set them in various issue silos; he extols their rights and legitimate claims to justice denied in the world. Yes, he proclaims such justice to be the actual work of Christ's church in this world and scatters crumbs behind him as he walks with his congregation on this journey through dense forests lest we who wish to follow might somehow lose our way.

Perhaps this is not the kind of book that one would expect to have been written by a comfortable, solidly upper-middle-class "white" man from an extraordinarily privileged background. This is not the kind of text that one would imagine a powerful former executive at the nation's largest bank to write. Perhaps that is why it is such an important work, for in addition to the content and theory of change that John proposes, he himself serves as an exemplar of one who is actively working to overcome the myopic gaze of white, male, cisgendered heteronormativity by fully immersing himself in the midst of Others and learning to value and love them with a pastoral heart.

Rev. Cleghorn has defined this congregation as the Island of Misfit Toys, referring to the holiday television classic featuring Rudolph the Red-Nosed Reindeer where discarded and abused lost toys were gathered away from the world. I might simply push back against this affectionate designation and say that never in any church have I felt more warmth, seen more joy, experienced a greater welcome, or been more at home. These "misfits" seem to fit well together and to manifest the Kingdom/Kindom of God far better than the members of many "fit" churches. The congregants really are not misfit toys; they are the essence of what the church should be! They are people many once (twice, thrice . . .) broken by a callous world governed by rules of exclusion and tendencies toward oppression who have found in Christ and in this place a sanctuary. This church is the proverbial safe port in the midst of a raging storm for many who might otherwise have lost their way. Here they find shelter. With each other they have found family; together they have found a happy home. What more could they ask for?

And Pastor John, a man who could easily have been the chosen pastor of the largest local big-steeple, mainline Presbyterian church, a man who would have been welcomed to oversee a monochromatic congregation with a multi-million-dollar budget and a healthy endowment, a man who could have quietly sat out the controversy over LGBTQ inclusion and migrant rights and Black Lives Matter, a man who would be a natural fit to shepherd the thousands at a Covenant Presbyterian Church, has found his ministry in a campus of small buildings containing a faith community of a few hundred intersecting oppressed and marginalized people on the edge of Uptown Charlotte. And what more would he ask for?

Rev. Rodney S. Sadler Jr., PhD
July 2020

INTRODUCTION

One of my questions for God when we meet face to face will be why are we such a doggone tribal people?

I know the experts say it is our tribal instincts that have kept us alive over the eons. But those same instincts sure cause a lot of trouble these days. The church has wrestled with this same dilemma since Christ called it together, and Paul and Peter began to organize Christ's followers. Even the apostles disagreed mightily at times about who should be in or out and why.

After the surprise of being called to serve as pastor to one of my denomination's most diverse congregations, I've been looking for answers ever since. This book is about that search.

Two decades ago, pastors and scholars wrote several shelves of books focused on the idea of "multiculturalism." That made perfect sense then. America and the mainline Protestant church were grasping its multicolored and multicultural future amid the advance of globalism and more fluid immigration patterns. That future America is here now, and the conversation about its implications grips our public dialogue.

But, while America is being transformed, its mainline Protestant churches are not. We're still sorted and separated in many different ways. The church continues to grapple with how to be inclusive and reflective of all God's children, struggling with both language and practice in its pursuit of diversity. Coming from the perspective of being white and cisgender, a majority of church leaders haven't broken the code on racial integration despite the contributions of scholars and practitioners in all those books written twenty years ago and up to today. The racial diversity mainline Protestant churches do have tends to exist in silos in homogeneous congregations. Not only that, what multiculturalism often left out was consideration of the full welcome of the LGBTQ community. Socioeconomic diversity in a given congregation is equally rare.

Building on the now somewhat dated idea of multiculturalism, a few scholars lately have begun to consider how various minority and oppressed populations can intersect in church with each other and the white majority. A few books have explored the theory of that question. This book takes the next step. It draws from the dynamic lives of the handful of churches in one major Protestant denomination, the Presbyterian Church (USA),[1] where America's near-future diversity, in all its permutations, is lived out every day.

In cities where white folks are already the racial minority and where urban progressives make up more and more of the populace, these congregations know the liberation of resurrection. At one time or another, each got close enough to the tomb to glance inside before choosing the road less traveled and following it to new possibilities, growth, and fresh dynamics in ministry.

Resurrection is a powerful thing. Just ask Jesus. This book shares the wondrous and sometimes bumpy journeys of these unusually diverse, vibrant, and missional congregations, following the hills and valleys, straightaways and dangerously sharp turns that come on the road these congregations deliberately chose. These congregations intersect differing races and ethnicities, sexual orientations and identities, socioeconomic categories, neighborhoods, religious backgrounds, and many other shades of difference with which God has blessed them.

As America moves relentlessly toward a vastly pluralistic destiny, the experiences of these congregations bear rich testimony to God's vision for a more just and diverse church, one that values and affirms all differences and centers those who are so often on the outside. These are the churches that chose against taking the highway. Instead, they stop and dwell at intersections, all kinds of intersections, where friends and strangers, the wounded and the healthy, and the insider and the outcast meet. Together they grow, heal, serve, practice radical hospitality, and seek God.

They explore the expanse of the audacious claim by the apostle Paul when he wrote to the gathered at Galatia: "As many of you as were baptized into Christ have clothed yourselves with Christ. There is no longer Jew or Greek, there is no longer slave or free, there is no longer male and female; for all of you are one in Christ Jesus."[2]

MY OWN LIBERATION

This is also the story of my own liberation. In many ways, I might be the poster child of the PC(USA) and even mainline Protestantism. I am white, straight, cisgender, privileged, educated, financially comfortable, and rich in social capital. If you extrapolate my age against the numerical decline of my denomination, assuming nothing with the church changes, I might be the one to turn the lights out in the PC(USA) before going on to God.

God has very different plans, of course. This book is about my ongoing education in what those plans might be.

It's about how the church might adapt to live into its calling to welcome, heal, and empower *all*, including centering "the other." It's about how the church must resist the potentially morphine-like effects of comfort and complacency to follow Jesus Christ. That path will require challenging structures and systems that fuel fear and drive division, those that resist the fulfillment of God's will for just and loving community in the name of short-term survival.

For leaders, thinkers and dreamers in mainline Protestant churches, including my beloved PC(USA), my prayer is these stories and examples might spur conversations about God's "what-if" for us too-often timid and tribal people.

How do we rediscover the meaning of resurrection?

THE FIRST CHURCH
OF THE ISLAND OF
MISFIT TOYS

On any given day, the sun rises, clears the neighborhood's soaring oaks, and sends its rays angling downward onto Caldwell Presbyterian Church. The first rays slip through the sanctuary's east windows and focus on a patch of pews. Like a spotlight, they declare, "Pay attention. Something is about to happen here." Then, slowly, the sunlight spreads pew by pew until it fills the entire sanctuary, as if the Holy Spirit has arrived and taken up residency.

On Sunday mornings, that first patch of sunlight is where our community begins to stir. About an hour before worship, the same few folks come early, when it is still quiet, to sit alone in the light with God for a few minutes. They come eager to sit not only in the warm embrace of that first patch of sunlight but also in the warm embrace of their church family. It is as odd, unlikely, and scrambled a bunch as one will find in any church in any city in America.

Peg, a white, cisgender professional, is often the first to arrive. At one time in her life, the very idea of being Presbyterian, much less an elder and a leader, would have caused her to erupt in sarcastic laughter. After running away from her stern Baptist upbringing in Alabama, she spent decades sampling all life offered. But her spirit never really stopped reaching back for God, and her God did not slumber. Later in life than most, she asked to be baptized. Now there she is on Sundays, straightening the hymnals and welcome cards in the pew racks, about the most unconventional "church lady" one can imagine.

Then into the light comes Jefforey, a handsome, African American man whose distinguished gray hair and straight-up bearing left over from his military days, belie the deep gentleness of his spirit. Often as not on Sundays, he wears his T-shirt emblazoned with the church's motto and promise, "God invites. We welcome. All." As with Peg, he felt drawn to God as a child in church, even to preach some in his teens. But religion's rejection of his sexual orientation as a gay man sent him on a long sojourn in the wilderness until he was able to feel welcomed, safe, and valued in church again.

Next, Ann arrives, usually looking as stylish and subtly sophisticated as one may expect of a retired banking executive from California. White and cisgender, her job relocated her to the South, but now she does a lot of church work in retirement. Charlotte is her home largely because church is her community, one that meets her desire for growth in faith and her hunger for justice. Then into the spreading sunlight of community comes Johnny, a gay Southern gentlemen whose big frame matches his outsized personality and joy in life. All of that was almost lost to his demons a few years ago, but his faith and his friends pulled him through.

His pew mate Linda Ellen is white and cis. As her double

first name hints, she grew up in a small Southern town but found herself yearning for something more from church. Next to her is in the pew is Eddy, a former Roman Catholic, Cuban-born business professional who came out as a gay man after having a family. He clung to his faith while suffering through a time of separation from his children, but he is now joyfully reunited with them and gives endlessly of his time in response to God's abiding grace through his journey.

One by one they come—Black and white and brown, rich and poor and middle class, gay and straight and trans—from dozens of neighborhoods across the city and metro region. The sunlight fans out to all corners of the sanctuary, and the pews fill with this rag-tag gaggle—disciples, seekers, skeptics, and the few remaining senior saints who never gave up on their old church, even as it prepared to close its doors a few years back. They rejoiced when God answered their prayers to save the church, even if those answers came in forms and fashions they would have never imagined or, perhaps, requested.

As members chat and visitors are greeted, Ruby slips in through the side entrance and head straight to the choir room. Perhaps today they will sing the old gospel, "I'm Coming Up the Rough Side of the Mountain," words she has surely lived as she struggled with poverty most of her life.

At about 10:50 a.m., Fred rises from his usual spot toward the front where he has been greeting friends and visitors. Hobbled but never stopped by the neuropathy that has taken away the feelings in his toes, he steps into the bell tower. In his working years, he was a senior engineer for both a major national airline and a cruise ship company. Since the church's unlikely resurrection, he focuses those considerable skills on the church's sometimes demon-possessed HVAC systems. More important, on Sundays, he is also the official bell ringer, a duty he embraces with the joy of a child with a new toy. Fred pulls hard on the rope and the seven-hundred-pound brass bell in the tower fifty feet above slowly begins to swing and sway, gaining momentum until it sends a clarion call to all who would come to worship.

The interracial gospel choir forms in the rear of the sanctuary to kick off worship. They sing the first strains of "I've Got a Feeling Everything's Gonna Be All Right" and process down the center aisle. Wide-eyed children in their parents' arms and curious visitors turn to see what all the commotion is about. At a place that's been called the First Presbyterian Church of the Island of Misfit Toys, it's time for worship.

NEW THINGS IN FORGOTTEN PLACES

In cities across America, on corners and blocks where abundance and scarcity have swapped places over the decades, God is resurrecting the church in unexpected ways. The prophet Isaiah might call it a "new thing."

As thousands of so-called mainline Protestant Christians count the dollars and the days before their churches close the doors for good, esteemed elders and Sunday school stalwarts in other places are scooting down from their usual spot in the pew. They graciously yield more than just their favorite vantage point for Sunday worship. They are yielding power. Joining them is a most unlikely mix of believers and seekers—from many races, gender identities, and sexual orientations, as well as many socioeconomic classes and religious paths.

The newcomers bring their dreams of social justice and

their hopes for life-giving community. Many bring their wounds, disappointments, and questions about God. They bring their doubts and suspicions about the church and organized religion. What these newcomers share, however, is a stubborn desire to be in relationship with God and a resilient curiosity about what the God they came to love and long for years ago still may do. They yearn for a church that won't shrink from hard conversations. They cling to a belief in a church that one day might live into its call to stand in the gap for those whom the broader culture loves to judge, leave behind, and step on in its fever of radical individualism and dream hoarding.

Many of these seekers and wary returnees go out of their way to get to church. They drive past more established churches with full program schedules and equally full parking lots on Sunday mornings and Wednesday nights. They walk into buildings long past their glory days, sanctuaries where the paint is peeling, the plaster is cracked, and members make do in poorly lit fellowship halls with kitchens equipped generations ago. They come and commit to a "comfort zone" that isn't always so comfortable, where the fruits of authentic diversity—namely constructive tension and glorious messiness—define the norm. In these often overlooked and forgotten places, they trust Jesus enough to be vulnerable and to reach for solidarity across difference, despite the risks that come with authentic diversity.

At these crossroads, there is resurrection and new life in unexpected forms.

People stretch and sometimes stumble. Leaders fail, but at least they hope to fail forward. Wounds sometimes close. Other times, they tear open a bit when an honest attempt at candor goes wrong, when hurt feelings and frayed trust are the price paid in pursuit of genuine relationship in Christ.

Still, God shows up in ways that may just chart a path forward for congregations caught in the swirl of demographic shifts and cultural cyclones whistling just outside the church doors.

For decades, church leaders and thinkers, often a step behind, have used a range of terms, concepts, and labels to describe diverse churches. In the middle part of the twentieth century, they were first called "integrated" churches. Then came "multiracial," "multicultural," "intercultural" church, and so on as America grew into its pluralism.

Call this newest "new thing" the intersectional church, borrowing an idea from the academy's study of gender, identity, and power.[1] It's an idea rooted in the truth that no one is just one thing, that each person blends identity and experience in distinct ways. A powerful tool for those with and without power, intersectionality considers how people in multiple marginalized groups are affected by systemic and institutional forms of prejudice and oppression. Pioneered in the 1990s, intersectionality has shed new light in law, politics, the academy, community organizing, and other areas. Only now are scholars beginning to consider what intersectionality has to offer the church.

Kimberlé Crenshaw, the Columbia University professor who originated intersectional analysis, rooted the idea in several groundbreaking lawsuits and papers, including the case of two African American women who sued their employer for discrimination. They claimed two-fold discrimination—on the basis of their gender and on the basis of their race. Intersectionality looks at power and privilege from the margins and asks: How are systems and institutions compounding oppression and mistreatment of those who are in more than one group or identity? How can we build new institutions that reflect both the new America and God's hunger for a kin-dom on earth defined by God's idea of justice and peace?

I should readily acknowledge I fit none of the oppressed groups that intersectional thinking has in mind. I am a cis-gender, straight, white, educated, privileged, affluent male with three degrees and deep social capital. Raised as upper middle class, I have been around power my entire life and navigate its halls comfortably. That means I am complicit in the sins of power and privilege. Looking the part with pre-mature white hair, I succeeded in two careers in the private sector spanning twenty-five years before entering ministry. I am not who scholars and theologians have in mind when they write about the dire need for a broader intersectional understanding in our society. If anything, I look like those who may have quite different interests than those whom intersectional thinking seeks to help.

But God's calling and gift to serve the church I pastor has changed all of that. For fourteen years, I have served and come to love those whose lives look very different from mine. They have allowed me to walk with them through the pain of their rejection based on sexual identity. They have allowed me to see the sting of racism and the weight of generational poverty through their eyes. They have shared their journeys with mental illness, trauma, and depression. They have invited me along as they go through gender tran-sition. They have let me sit with them as they waited faith-fully and patiently for their children to embrace them again after coming out. They educate me as more and more inter-racial couples bring their children, hoping to find a church that better resembles the world those kids will inherit. They welcome the people who sleep in the city park behind the church with a warm greeting, a hug, and an offer of help when we pass the peace.

A New Way Forward?

Twenty-eight years after she coined the term "intersectionality," Kimberlé Crenshaw explained it in these ways:

> Intersectionality is a lens through which you can see where power comes and collides, where it interlocks and intersects. It's not simply that there's a race problem here, a gender problem here, and a class or LBGTQ problem there. Many times, that framework erases what happens to people who are subject to all of these things.[2]

This book asks: Can congregations apply intersectionality as a new lens amid unprecedented social diversity that recasts the mainline Protestant church from being mostly white, cisgender, and middle class? Can the tool of intersectionality strengthen the church in its service to Jesus Christ as his body? How can a more intersectional understanding by Christ's servants help them deliver justice, level the mountains that separate us, and make straight the paths that divide us?

I need to acknowledge I am stretching the core idea of intersectionality. While they are highly diverse for the mainline Protestant, the churches that helped with this work are, except for one, majority white in their congregational makeup. If intersectionality were to be applied purely to demographics, only one of these congregations fits the mold as being majority people of color, female, and more than marginal in their LGBTQ membership. The rest of the congregations considered are majority white in makeup, and most are led by white, cisgender men as clergy. I am attempting to use the idea of intersectionality as Crenshaw intended, as a tool for analysis to consider what is happening in PC(USA) churches that, even though majority white, have the most intersectional diversity. In a sense, then, these congregations give us some early indicators of what the future church may be like.

Some may say intersectional thinking and theology make for an odd dancing partner with the Reformed theology that anchors the Protestant tradition. However, my reading and attempts to envision intersectionality as a type of liberation theology have enlivened and enlightened my faith, preaching, and teaching.

As sure as the church at large needs historic voices such as John Calvin, Martin Luther, and Karl Barth as cornerstones, we need to hear emerging minority voices as we seek to invite today's and tomorrow's America into our pews. But this book is not just about evangelism in the twenty-first century. It's about an awakening that is in reach for church leaders at all levels and the congregations they serve. It's an invitation to experience God in Christ and the Spirit in new ways for contemporary disciples—but ways that echo the experience of the marginalized, first-century church.

My growing awareness of all of this drove the years of research that stand behind this book. I am grateful to those who have previously written about ideas like the multicultural church and who have opened their reading of Scripture and practice of faith to include, rather than exclude, the LGBTQ community. I am grateful to denominational leaders and conference speakers who have wrestled with years of incremental improvements in diversity within church membership and haven't stopped.

I know some thought leaders in this area of study and practice will be quick to cite flaws in this book and in my interpretation. The dialogue about intersectionality and social justice moves swiftly, and in some cases I may have fallen behind already. I welcome the feedback. (For example, in the opening line of this book I used the word "tribal" to describe the human tendency to seek shelter, company, and affirmation from those most like us. Since writing that line, I've learned the word *tribal* carries its own baggage and can be used to denigrate those of Latinx heritage and culture. I meant no disrespect.)

I am deeply encouraged by the strong forward progress my denomination, the PC(USA), has made in the last two to three years in shifting its leadership, policy, theology, and teaching to be far more inclusive and justice oriented. Other mainline Protestant denominations, each working through their own polity, are at their own points in this journey, some ahead and others behind in terms of inclusivity. The teachers and examples I've encountered inform my efforts, as halting and imperfect as they are, to live into these possibilities and to navigate their risks as an ordained minister of word and sacrament.

The major thrust of this book is two-fold: first, to point out that we, the church, have an enormous amount of work to do to open God's church more widely, and second, to point to congregations and their leaders who are living all of this out in daily, intersectional, "both/and" life together.

In these places, perhaps not by name per se, the intersectional church has been taking shape. Often in overlooked and forgotten neighborhoods—such as Baltimore; Atlanta; Brooklyn; Charlotte; Pittsburgh; Washington, DC; Denver; suburban Chicago; and Detroit—God is fueling a unique expression, energy, and re-creation. This path can inform congregations yearning to heat up our old, beloved, frozen-chosen ways.

These congregations are almost all urban and historic churches. In many cases, their initial congregations largely moved away to the suburbs or slowly died off. Many others, having flirted with death, found new life in taking risk and experimentation. One church pastor refers to his church's lean times and its transformational effect as when "the church grew small."

These congregations' understanding of mission is shaped by progressive theology that bears witness to their members' diversity and experience with marginalization. God's call for justice serves as the center post of their outreach and advocacy in Christ. They think of themselves as spiritual hospitals for wounded souls. They mix LGBTQ members who love God but know the rejection of church with those openly living with depression or various other forms of mental illness, those whose lives are bent by institutional racism, those in recovery, and those who put a high premium on diversity in church.

In turn, because they involve those once on the outside looking in, these congregations practice innovative new forms of leadership development, governance, and decision-making. They seek to challenge, if not deconstruct, white heterosupremacy in practice and in polity. They recognize traditional church polity but know its limits (and sometimes push those limits). They welcome its check-and-balance function but worry about rules outweighing relationships in importance.

Worship in these intersectional churches is joyful, flexible, fluid, and inclusive, blending traditional music with other styles, be it jazz, Black gospel, or global. Current events, whether national or local, find their way into liturgy, sermon, and prayers. While reformed, these Presbyterian flocks practice a wide theology that emphasizes radical hospitality, inclusive grace, and the call of the church to act as the body of Christ in the world.

To welcome all in worship, intersectional churches stretch their pew sitters' experience on a weekly basis, on purpose. A mark of their idea of success is everyone is likely to find at least one element of worship unfamiliar, if not a little uncomfortable. They think of evangelism as bearing public witness. Social justice and inclusion anchor not just their "mission outreach" but also their entire identity—from governance to congregational care, from education offerings to worship, from theology to how they use their buildings.

Intersectional worship is not necessarily for the casual Christian who seeks a church where they can worship on Sundays, come and go easily, and encounter only what is comfortable, familiar, and unchallenging. The possibilities that come with being an intersectional church also bring plenty of potential pitfalls. Preachers and worship leaders lacking in pastoral agility and the ability to self-differentiate should think twice. Those seeking to avoid being bumped and bruised—but also deeply changed in their faith—need not apply. Take my word. I will show you my bumps and bruises, but also gladly testify about liberation.

But amid this gloriously messy, faith-deepening adventure, there is a new way forward for the church that has largely failed to respond to Rev. Dr. Martin Luther King Jr.'s frequent observation that the worship hour is America's most segregated. God invites her church to this "new thing" that looks like the old thing, the first-century church that was initially a movement of outcasts and allies, skeptics and questioners, the wounded and the weary in need of grace, love, and justice.

2

WHAT HAPPENS
AT INTERSECTIONS

Funny things happen at intersections. Things you're not expecting. But isn't that God's way? In an age when the masters of our coming and going by car design everything to maximize speed, ease, and efficiency of movement, God seems to love intersections to slow us down and cause encounter. More than multilane freeways that keep us in silos or traffic circles that keep us circling each other cautiously at safe distances, God has a way of putting intersections where we would only otherwise tap our brakes and stay in our lane.

I was, I thought, in the fast lane to a traditional kind of church, maybe as an associate pastor at one of the local churches that fierce Scots-Irish settlers founded centuries ago in what became my city of Charlotte. Maybe I would go to one of the city's more affluent and thriving white, urban churches bankers, lawyers, and other professionals join to raise their kids in the faith of their parents. After all, I was already in their lane. Those were my people. If not that, then perhaps one of the suburban or other churches in the Charlotte region could use someone like me.

Twenty years earlier, I'd come to Charlotte as a reporter for the daily newspaper, following in my father's footsteps. Then I traded my reporter's notebook for a dark suit and patterned tie to go to work for the leaders of one of the region's fast-rising banks. In the 1980s, interstate banking laws had opened the path to what would become today's coast-to-coast financial giants. I was offered the chance to apply my background in writing, communicating, and storytelling to introduce a bank that would be a new and pivotal player in cities across the southeastern United States as it bought one bank after another.

The work spoke to my interest in civic affairs and leadership. I knew the top executives at the bank came from various backgrounds and cared deeply for communities and people. The opportunity to work directly for the chief executive officer offered me a way to use power for the public good. Next came marriage and a mortgage, then a child and a second, each a gift and a responsibility. When I wasn't working or spending time with family, I channeled energy to my church and some of the city's nonprofits that were focused on solving Charlotte's ills.

But God kept putting up yield signs, caution signals, and flashing lights, even a speed bump or two, saying, "Don't get too comfortable. I know the plans I have for you." God, seminary, and the church and I flirted, at times seriously, winking at each other as my wife, Kelly, and I raised a family. I served as an elder at an influential "purple" church (one balancing a range of theological and political views) and a vineyard worker in the city I came to love. Life was full, busy, and rich.

Then, when the Presbyterian saints in Charlotte conspired with Union Presbyterian Seminary to open a second campus specifically for second-career entrants in ministry, I got down on my knees. The bank I'd joined a decade earlier had grown fifty-fold from a regional US company into a global giant. The broad-minded, inspirational leaders I'd felt called to work with had retired. My wife and I huddled and decided to at least take the first step. The new seminary branch operated on weekends, so I could study and keep a paycheck. I said a prayer, checked my mirrors, and hit my turn signal to take what would be a five-year-long exit ramp out of corporate life preparing for ministry . . . somewhere.

Even then, I thought I had it all mapped out. Upon graduation with a master of divinity degree, I figured God would place me in a church like most that my privileged bubble had ever shown me. It would probably be like the one that shaped me as a youth in Atlanta—white, affluent, involved in the community, writing checks, taking mission trips, and spending a few Saturdays a year building Habitat for Humanity homes or working in food pantries. I had the course laid out and marked in red marker on the map. The financial plan added up. I didn't really *have* to sing along with that country hit, "Jesus, Take the Wheel." I *had* this.

Isn't that the way?

I was, unwittingly, part of the problem we have created in America, staying in my lane, only vaguely aware of how my privilege shaped everything I knew. I was comfortably cognizant of the painful struggle my neighbors across town faced daily against systems and institutions built to favor me and mine. I loved God and my church, but it, too, was staying it its lane, I realize now. Presbyterians hanging with Presbyterians, for the most part. White folks with white folks, Black folks with Black folks, interrupted by the rare and well-intended church-partnership with different folks. Any LGBTQ folks I knew in church in those days stayed in the closet.

What I didn't see was how we were only driving past each other, our separated neighborhoods and the stories the houses there told about how we all lived our lives separate, apart, and unequal. And so it was for our country, too, and my church. My native PC(USA) was struggling with the issue of same-gender marriage in the 1990s. I worked with and knew a few LGBTQ folks but never really internalized the truth of their struggle, including their often-tortuous relationship with the church.

At an early age, I'd learned from my father, a civil rights journalist, about the truth of racial discrimination—and how far people with power and privilege will go to keep it, to keep others down. I'd also learned collaborative justice and restoration work is murky and sometimes has unintended consequences. As a younger man, I'd worked through a church partnership in a declining neighborhood where African American families and senior citizens were trying to stabilize and reclaim their neighborhood from the drug houses and hopelessness that encroached. Our work in that neighborhood made a difference and it felt good—at the time.

Twenty years later, I mourn that our best intentions inadvertently helped set the stage for the gentrification that today is pushing poorer and middle-class neighbors out of our affluent and too-often unmindful city. Meanwhile, though, I was making good time in my fast-lane pursuit of what I just knew God had in store for me. After completing seminary, I'd leave the bank as a forty-one-year old senior vice president and slide right into the ministry. No muss, no fuss.

My wife, Kelly, never signed up for any of this, nor did our children. But they provided the grace and wide space to let me follow this crazy dream, even if our daughters saw less of me as I studied Greek, Hebrew, theology, and church history every Saturday. I continued to tell myself it could work. I presumed I knew the plans God had for me. The lane was clear as long as I kept my foot on the gas, faced forward, and didn't look around too much.

THE INTERSECTION OF PARK AND FIFTH . . . AND MORE

Then God put in an intersection. Full stop. It's the joke, which is truth too: "If you want to make God laugh, tell God your plans." Prior to finishing seminary, as I attended to my duties at the bank, I used all my social capital to let the world know I would soon be available for ministry. And I waited. I had this. No sweat.

I was clueless to the story that was unfolding at an old church just a few blocks from my home. In twenty years of active work at Covenant Presbyterian Church and in the local presbytery, I'd never heard of Caldwell Memorial Presbyterian Church. Because it was dying a long, slow, invisible death.

In my fast lane, I'd driven right past it but never noticed it.

If I had noticed it, to be perfectly honest, I confess—in my naive, blind ideas about what God can do—I would have figured it had nothing to offer me. On its last legs and last dollars, having been carried by a dwindling handful of faithful, aging, blue-haired Presbyterians, it was not the kind of place God would put me. There was nothing there. Even the Presbytery was hovering, in need of the cash value of the land close to center city. The Presbytery had shot itself in the foot with huge financial losses. It had a bet on purchasing a property for the next big church in the exurbs, following the "same-old" model of chasing mostly white, affluent suburbanites.

But God was there, at the long-forgotten intersection of Park and Fifth Streets, in one of the city's first streetcar suburbs now a mile and a half from the center of this booming city. The remaining few senior saints at Caldwell, who had watched so many of their friends leave or die, had pulled the last rabbit out of the hat. In their struggle to revive the church—and, later, just keep the lights on—they'd raided the organ repair fund to pay the power bill and the pittance of a salary for part-time Rev. Dr. Charles MacDonald and a part-time office assistant. Dr. MacDonald was the esteemed, seventy-eight-year old pastor supplied by the Presbytery who had done everything he could to keep the church going. The church was out of money, options, ideas, and energy. There was nothing left.

Caldwell Memorial's board of elders sent the letter to Presbytery to close the church.

God chuckled and began to reveal the real plan, one that had begun a half-century earlier.

In its heyday, as one of the city's leading Presbyterian churches, Caldwell helped start many other churches to meet the growing city's spiritual needs. This was a particular passion of Caldwell patriarch William Henry Belk. Many US cities had a William Henry Belk. As the South grew, Belk was a master merchant who was building a highly successful chain of department stores in the Carolinas, Tennessee, and Virginia. Belk was also a devout Presbyterian who postponed his own baptism as a young adult because he considered himself not worthy of God's grace and not ready for the responsibility that grace bestowed. Fortunately, for the church at large and for Caldwell, he came around.

Henry Belk loved to help new churches get a start. As World War II came to an end, he and others at Caldwell planted a church about a mile northeast of the city across the street from a sprawling, new public housing development that had been built with returning war veterans in mind. Seigle Avenue Presbyterian opened as a white church serving the then-new public housing development, Piedmont Courts, which was filling up with returning white war veterans. Decades later, amid the tectonic shifts of the 1960s, suburban sprawl, white flight, and government neglect took hold of the Piedmont Courts area. Low-income African Americans moved in looking for affordable housing. The property value in the surrounding neighborhood slumped.

The members of Seigle Avenue Presbyterian faced a choice. Stay put or move to the suburbs, as thousands of churches did across the country in those years. Seigle remained and became a beacon of integration and urban ministry. In time, the church's compassion and care for the residents of Piedmont Courts attracted a mix of members—African Americans from Piedmont Courts served by Seigle's preschool, afternoon youth program, and spirited worship; and affluent, progressive white folk. Some came from Myers Park Presbyterian, a congregation of bankers, lawyers, merchants, and civic leaders that also financially supported Seigle Avenue.

Through the 1970s and 1980s, Seigle Avenue Presbyterian and the residents of Piedmont Courts intertwined their lives around the worship and service of God. New church members still came, attracted by the diversity, inclusivity, and genuine welcome, including some LGBTQ people in the 1990s and early 2000s who felt the love and authentic mission that radiated from the place. The Rev. Charlie

Summers balanced the church's many interests and person-alities and became well loved for his authentic approachabil-ity and preaching.

In those years, the members of Seigle didn't know it, but they were practicing what Kimberlé Crenshaw had begun to call "intersectionality." Its members openly shared their faith, their lives, their struggles, and their victories as they deconstructed what traditional church leadership looked like and brought in those who had only been on the outside of church life.

But, ultimately, it did not hold. The congregation later fractured. Much of the membership scattered, many search-ing but not finding another diverse church. God's truth in Ecclesiastes 3 about there being "a time for everything" set-tled in. The diaspora of those who left Seigle found other churches—or none—as they mourned what was lost.

A few years passed. Later, former members of the well-known Seigle Gospel Choir, long led by professional musi-cian Smitty Flynn, were asked to come back together to sing at the opening convocation of Charlotte's Queens Univer-sity. The reunion sparked interest in the members of the Seigle diaspora finding other reasons to gather. Some began meeting for Bible study. Needing a place to convene, they heard about a church that might have spare room, one they knew little about. It was named Caldwell Memorial Presby-terian Church.

In fall 2006, two things were happening at the corner of Park and Fifth Streets in Charlotte. The leaders at Caldwell were realizing they could not keep the church doors open. The Seigle diaspora, on the other hand, found new life and vigor together as they huddled in a borrowed room at Cald-well on Sunday nights, shared a meal, and studied progressive, mission-oriented theology. They came to realize how much they missed being part of a faith community of faith.

On their own, Tovi and Kevin Martin, members of the Seigle Avenue diaspora, began visiting Caldwell's Sunday worship. A young, interracial couple, they were warmly greeted by the ten to fifteen remaining members who were white and elderly. The couple appreciated Dr. MacDonald's intellectual but challenging sermons and were taken by the charm of the old sanctuary, where flaking ceiling plaster sometimes fell in worshippers' laps but the Spirit was clearly felt.

"The first time I actually attended worship at Caldwell was Easter Sunday, 2005," recalled Kevin Martin. "The first thing I noticed was that no one turned their head or batted an eye when my wife and I, this random interracial couple, showed up."

"They were all about seventy years old or so, and you might not have expected as welcoming a group of people to a nontraditional couple as Kevin and me," added Tovi Martin, accustomed to feeling stares when she and her husband were out. "They were very welcoming each time we came, not just in saying the words but in their engagement with us. That was very comforting."

That same fall 2006, Kevin felt called to join Caldwell, despite the folly of joining a dying church where everyone looked different from him. But on the very next Sunday, Dr. MacDonald announced the church would close.

"I thought, 'Man, my timing is not the best in the world,'" he said.

After talking with the Martins, Dr. MacDonald and the handful of elders who made up the governing session saw one last chance. One of those elders, then in her late eighties, was Jackie Abernethy. She had grown up at Caldwell, seen it soar and then fade. She had reconciled herself to its closing but agreed with Dr. MacDonald that God just might be up to something.

"Kevin said he was going to call some of his friends and they were going to come Sunday," Jackie said. "So, I stood at the door and they just kept coming and coming."

In September and October 2006, as word spread among the former Seigle members about the "new thing" God was doing at Park and Fifth, attendance at Caldwell picked up. Years after they had been together, people of different colors, classes, and sexual identities came in short sleeves and blue jeans with hurts, doubts, addictions, and questions, but most of all, with a deep need for community.

They found the somewhat formal, old folks in simple dresses and coats and ties greeted them with authentic welcomes and unconditional hospitality. One of these old folks, Jimmy Todd, a mostly retired businessman and a son of influence, took his post as usher on the day a few former members of Seigle planned to visit. As he greeted the growing flow of visitors and handed out worship bulletins, he realized what was necessary for his beloved old church to survive and to give way to God.

"There was fifty of them and only one of me," he said later. "I thought I'd better be the one to do the changing."

With those words, vastly different than the refrain at so many dying churches, Caldwell's life cycle took a strange and unlikely turn. The child returned to care for the parent and God's unimaginable plan moved on.

Over several months, the newcomers and the Caldwell remnant charted a new way forward together. It can hardly be overstated how important it was that the senior citizens who made up the old Caldwell remnant did not force any idols on the newcomers. They did not present a list of "dos and don'ts" or impose restrictions rooted in those words that have killed so many churches: we've never done it that way. They trusted God.

DO YOU BELIEVE IN MIRACLES?

On Easter morning 2007, the *Charlotte Observer* devoted most of its front page to what it declared to be "The Miracle on Fifth Street." That morning, a couple of dozen people around the city woke up, read the paper over coffee, came to Easter worship at Caldwell to hear the good news of Christ's resurrection, and found a new church home.

Dr. MacDonald, and a revised session (leadership group) representing the new mix, did something remarkable, suturing together different worship styles, theologies, and ideas about community mission. Neither group went for praise music. The old Caldwell folks loved to sing traditional hymns, which they often knew by heart. The newcomers drew life from Black gospel music that reminded them of their role in God's unfinished business of racial justice. The Caldwell remnant loved to pass the peace for five to ten minutes, roaming the sanctuary to hug and embrace. The Seigle diaspora loved to share their joys and concerns, large and small, and even testify every now and then before the prayer for the people. Under Dr. MacDonald's leadership, they wove these traditions together to create a blended worship experience. Also, they joyfully made plans to accommodate infants and youth in a space that had not heard the laughter of children in decades.

As a first piece of business, however, they gathered over several evenings to talk about the church's mission. They looked across a city with hundreds of healthy churches and asked themselves what was missing and what kind of church they would want to attend if it could be built from scratch.

Out of those conversations, a new mission statement declared their aspiration.

We seek to hear God's call not only as individuals but also as a progressive, missional community striving to reflect the kingdom of God in the here and now.

We embrace the rich history of the Reformed tradition and the storied past of our once-prominent, center-city church as we welcome a diverse, urban community of seekers—young and old, gay and straight, rich and poor—of all races and ethnicities.

We are called into meaningful, transformative community that values the unique blessings and perspectives of each member and offers a place of welcome and healing to weary souls.

We seek dynamic servant leaders who serve humbly, embrace change, and boldly challenge injustices in the wider community.

Most important, we seek to proclaim the gospel in both word and deed, following the life and teaching of Jesus Christ, our Lord and Savior.

THANK GOD FOR UNANSWERED PRAYERS

God was not through with me and my arrogance, either.

The career map for ministry I had marked so carefully and presumptively, the path I had tried to impose on God, became another reminder of who is really in charge. I'd been hungry for any ministry experience I could gain. A dear and wise woman, ninety-year-old Sarah Belk Gambrell, the only daughter of department store chain founder Henry Belk, had donated money to help start the seminary I was attending. We became loosely acquainted. She suggested I get to know Dr. MacDonald—having no idea what God was up to at Caldwell—because she thought he could be a mentor as someone who'd also entered ministry in midlife.

I dropped by to see him just as God had stuck her foot in the door of Caldwell's tomb. A few weeks later, he invited me to be a twenty-hour-a-week, unpaid assistant to the pastor. I kept my job at the bank and squeezed in church wherever I could.

When Dr. MacDonald saw God's vision for the place, he recommended the church form a pastor nominating committee to call a full-time leader. It was the first of many risky and courageous steps the small group would take. Even more risky was their decision to call me to be their pastor.

Who was to say that a rookie would find something several experienced predecessors had not, namely how to sustain the reversal after years and years of decline? Why not get a younger man or, even better, call a woman or a person of color to mark a new day for this diverse gaggle? Would the congregation expect Kelly to be a traditional "pastor's wife," something she did not invite? Would the family financial plan survive an 80 percent cut in my compensation? If you want to make God laugh, tell God *your* questions!

When God put me in that intersection as their new pastor in April 2008, rather than all the places I'd envisioned, I thought of Garth Brooks's song, "Thank God for Unanswered Prayers."

So, with wonder, trepidation, and a lot of prayer, I emptied my office at the bank and moved into the pastor's office at Caldwell. Rather than looking out over Uptown Charlotte's sparkling skyline through the tinted glass of the sixty-story bank tower, I took a seat at the heavy wooden pastor's desk in a dusty old office where God's light shone through 1914 stained-glass windows. Like the people beginning to become a congregation there, those windows were chipped, cracked, bowed, and bent by time and decades of neglect.

Since it was built in 1914 just one block away from the then-new mule-drawn trolley, the intersection of Fifth and Park in Charlotte has seen life come and go and come again. Now, a new convergence of twenty-first-century wounded seekers and weary believers of all types were beginning life together with a handful of senior saints who couldn't believe their eyes as the church came back to life. My education at seminary was over. My education under God and the odd flock that now called Caldwell home was just beginning.

I said a prayer and held on for dear life.

IS ANYONE OUT THERE?

My mother taught me to ask at every juncture in life: What is the highest and best use of my God-given abilities and experiences as I understand them right now?

At age twenty-two, that question led me to take up the newspaper business. I considered it as my first calling since it was the sum of my interests and skills and it served an important public interest. My father was a newspaper editor in Atlanta, Charlotte, and Detroit, before becoming dean of the University of Maryland College of Journalism. I appreciated the role of journalism in democracy, of shedding light where needed, of providing checks and balances to power, and of gathering and telling stories. My training in college and six years of writing more than one thousand stories for the *Charlotte Observer* taught me to gather the facts and the context for understanding them.

Following the resurrection at Caldwell, twenty-five years after my start as a rookie reporter, I found myself as a rookie pastor in a highly complex ministry context, a venture whose outcome remained in question. I needed all the facts and context I could gather, even as I began marrying, burying, baptizing, preaching, teaching, and helping create, alongside the dedicated lay leadership, a sustainable "new" church.

I also needed to know what I didn't know. Part of my tenure in banking related to risk management, which is the core business of any bank. Banks like to be paid back and are good at knowing what risks stand in the way of that. I didn't take up ministry to practice that kind of fiduciary risk management (if anything, I was taking on too much risk as the world might define it). But I was keenly aware of the need to be a good steward of what God had done at Caldwell.

Theologically, I subscribe to an outlook of abundance rather than scarcity—a conviction that a sovereign and just God is working things out according to the divine will, even in times of adversity and need. But God also calls us to be wise stewards. I was so convinced God had given us at Caldwell such a rare and precious gift. As with Moses, I prayed for the guidance I needed, fully aware of my lack of readiness. God had delivered me thus far. Now, I needed information and a broader perspective for this wondrous new and risky calling.

THE MOST SEGREGATED HOUR

Arriving at Caldwell was both a jump cut to the future and a vivid reminder of much of organized religion's failed progress in America. Rev. Dr. Martin Luther King Jr.'s insight about the dire segregation of Sunday mornings from his "Letter from a Birmingham Jail" is so often quoted today because of its stubborn endurance, especially in the so-called mainline or traditional Protestant church. On Sundays, for a wide range of reasons, we worship apart in silos and homogeneous groups. Meanwhile, the nation and the world look and act nothing like us.

America's hastening diversity and growing pluralism lies at the root of so much of the national experience—our debate about immigration, the terrifying and foreboding assertion of white supremacy, the ever-widening wealth gap, the drive for full equality for women and LGBTQ people, and on and on. The facts are clear and clearly visible. As reported by Axios in April 2019:

> By 2045, the US as a whole is projected to become majority minority. In other words, there will be no single racial or ethnic majority. America will be a patchwork quilt unlike any time in its history. Nonwhite Americans are now the majority of the population in four states, as well as in the most prosperous and powerful US cities.[1]

Despite the fear-driven and sometimes tragically violent protestations of many, the die is cast:

> Next year, the entire under-18 population will be majority nonwhite, according to William Frey, a Brookings Institution demographer and author of "Diversity Explosion: How New Racial Demographics are Remaking America." In less than a decade, the population under 30 will be majority nonwhite.[2]

Our cities are reaching this milestone much earlier as swift urbanization has reshaped the country. Witness my adopted hometown of Charlotte, once a quiet, predominantly white and Presbyterian town. Thirty-six metro areas are today majority minority, and eight have populations that comprise 75 percent minority populations.[3] Troublingly, a major part of our population greets this inevitability not with hope or a sense of possibility but with pessimism at best and fear at worst. America's latent racism showed in a 2019 Pew Research Center survey that found 59 percent of Republicans and 46 percent of white people said a majority non-white population will weaken American culture.[4]

Where is the mainline Protestant church in all of this? We are all staying in our lanes, avoiding eye contact with anyone around us, and accelerating toward a cliff even as America is losing confidence in the church.

In what was once known as a "Christian nation," white Christians now make up less than half of the US public. Only 43 percent of Americans identify as white and Christian and only 30 percent as white Protestant. The youngest religious groups in the US are Muslims, Buddhists, and Hindus. One in four Americans is religiously unaffiliated, a group that will certainly grow as older Americans die. One-third of millennials are religiously unaffiliated, and little seems to be reversing their disappointment and departure from organized religion.[5]

Alongside these changes in racial/ethnic diversity, America has become vastly more LGBTQ-welcoming, as reflected in the nation's increasing acceptance of same-gender marriage. Between 2001 and 2016, Pew Research Center polling showed the majority of Americans shifting from opposing same-gender marriage to supporting it.[6] In 2016, the United States judicial system had upheld same-gender marriage.

LGBTQ couples feature prominently today in television and print advertising as marketers seek to reach new buyers of products and services. As important, major corporations promote their progressive employment policies and dedicate big budgets to the recruitment and employee satisfaction of LGBTQ workers. These companies know diversity enriches their corporate culture and makes them more competitive.

But as the nation moved forward on diversity, mainline Protestant denominations stood still. The PC(USA)'s constitution, the Book of Order, calls congregations to seek "a new openness in its own membership, becoming in fact, as well as in faith, a community of women and men of all ages, races, ethnicities, and worldly conditions, made one in Christ by the power of the Spirit, as a visible sign of the new humanity."[7]

Yet the PC(USA), as a proxy of other mainline Protestant denominations, remains stubbornly 90 percent white in its membership, down just a percentage point or two from a decade ago. Even that progress was achieved indirectly. Thousands of white, more conservative congregations left the denomination over its broader acceptance of the LGBTQ community. Tens of thousands of the denomination's aging members die each year, and the COVID-19 pandemic will hasten the closing of congregations that were already struggling financially and otherwise.

So, for all of these reasons pastors and leaders at Presbyterian and other mainline churches would have no doubt about the need to build more diverse congregations, right? Not really.

A 2014 Lifeway Research study found 85 percent of senior pastors in mainline Protestant churches say every church should strive for racial diversity, but only 13 percent reported they have more than one predominant racial/ethnic group in their congregation. The same study found a similar disconnect among church members: 78 percent of all Americans say churches should strive for racial diversity but only 51 percent of churchgoers say they would be comfortable *even visiting* a church where there are multiple ethnicities represented.[8] We have a long, long way to go.

If the PC(USA) is a proxy for the mainline Protestant church, we don't seem to be leaving our lanes at all. In 2018, only 4 percent of congregations in the PC(USA) were multiracial, about the same as five years before, according to PC(USA) Research Services.

What diversity mainline Protestant denominations can claim exists on islands—African Americans worshipping and serving with African Americans, and the same for Latinx, Korean, and African Presbyterian congregations, respectively. The same is true in other mainline Protestant denominations in America. For many, the familiarity and homogeneity of these congregations are a comfort and an affirmation, which is why we need them. It's also true congregations of the same race or ethnicity can manifest *diversity of thinking* and ideas that stretch our faith and understanding of the gospel. That's important.

However, in light of the nation's deepening diversity, homogeneous congregations inherently limit how members experience each other's differing walks in life and experiences with the one God who gave us our splendid differences and whom we all serve and worship. There is little opportunity to understand all that goes with creating a more open and welcoming culture, as perceived and embraced by those in minority groups.

As for LGBTQ inclusion, we mainliners are doing no better. United Methodists in America are grappling with a rejection of equality driven mainly by international church representatives, not US pastors and lay leaders. Elsewhere, where progress with LGBTQ inclusion in the mainline Protestant church has occurred, it's been painfully slow. Presbyterians in North America, for example, began wrestling with questions related to homosexuality in the 1970s and the debate continued through and well beyond the reunification of the so-called Southern and Northern wings of Presbyterians in 1983, when the PC(USA) was formed from the merger. In the 1990s, the debate intensified with a series of overtures to the General Assembly dealing with the standards for ordination of teaching elders (pastors) and ruling elders (laity).

In 2011, a majority of the 173 presbyteries of the denomination approved a change in ordination standards to be more inclusive and welcoming. It allowed ordaining bodies (the elders) of individual churches to come to their own conclusion as to whether persons in same-gender relationships should be considered for ordination. In 2015, the denomination took the next step to amend its constitution's definition of marriage to include a "commitment between two people, traditionally a man and a woman," thus removing the final constitutional barrier to full inclusion of LGBTQ people.

Still, it's hard to know whether we are living out that promise to be more inclusive. Each year, the denomination requires congregations to fill out a statistical report that details the state of their church according to members gained or lost, the number of baptisms and children, budget information, and more. The report asks for information about the percentage of members who are women and who are of different races. By 2020, however, the denomination had not changed its annual statistical report to reflect LGBTQ membership. Thus, any effort to track the inclusion of LGBTQ members since the constitution changed is nearly impossible. I understand there are privacy and confidentiality issues involved and respect everyone's right to privacy. Sensitivity is important. That said, I remain curious how this don't-ask-don't-tell approach helps us measure our success.

So, we as a church have fallen far behind in keeping pace with our nation's demographic transformation. Now churches who seek diversity are faced with the questions of how to succeed in offering an authentic and full welcome to LGBTQ people, just as their employers, neighborhoods, Rotary clubs, and Scout troops are.

We have a steep hill to climb and it feels like I've been here before. Back in my banking days, while in San Francisco on a business trip, I decided to walk from the headquarters building to my hotel. It was only a few blocks, but those blocks climbed Nob Hill, which is a 25 percent grade. Walking up the first block, I felt myself getting winded as I hoofed along with my luggage in hand. At the top of the second block, with my heart pounding, I thought about calling for an ambulance. The sneaky thing about that short journey is the second block is steeper than the first.

This is similar to where the mainline Protestant church finds itself today. We have not found a way to deepen the racial integration of our church, and now we are called to be as inclusive of our LGBTQ friends and neighbors. The journey isn't easy. In fact, it's heart pounding. It's also not one everyone feels compelled to take. That many Christians prefer to worship surrounded by people who look like them is not an indictment, something I will explore in later chapters. But other congregations may yet hear the call to a more just and inclusive future.

Assata Zerai, current vice president of equity and inclusion at the University of New Mexico, spent a year researching diversity in the mainline Protestant church and came to these conclusions:

Literature focusing on multiracial churches, multicul-turalism and churches, and exclusion of LGBTIQ members has stalled in recent years. Times demand that we move beyond nominal demographic diver-sity—just letting difference in—to real inclusion, reflected in a church's values, mission, leadership, membership, and various aspects of its internal culture. To become an inclusive church takes embracing a social justice orientation. Such an orientation will drive members to learn about injustice in their commu-nities; it will necessitate their thinking with an inter-sectional lens to analyze their own social and spatial locations, and to unveil the ways each contributes to oppression. This orientation will encourage the hard conversations and difficult processes to break down privilege and eliminate marginalization.[9]

But we Presbyterians are formed and instructed by a consti-tution that calls for a new openness in the diversity of its members.

Each congregation must consider what that instruction means for its community and context. At Caldwell, given its unlikely resurrection, we were discerning a clear and focused calling to live out of its diversity full steam. God continues to push us to deeper understanding and learning about how to feed and nurture what we had.

Is There Anyone Else Like Us out There?

In my first years of ministry, I read all the books about diver-sity in the church. I attended all the conferences. Most, however, dealt with the idea of multicultural churches, defined as having at least 20 percent of their members from a nondominant race or ethnicity. These congregations blend white and African American worshippers and, in some cases, also with immigrants from places like Asia, Africa, and South and Central Americas. These contexts demand specific approaches and knowledge about everything from worship to pastoral care, but very rarely do they add the LGBTQ element.

As my earliest months and years at Caldwell passed, I found myself asking with more frequency, "Is there anyone else like us out there?"

Researchers use the benchmark of 20 percent as a measure for what is more than a marginal influence on the culture and dynamics of a congregation. So, with America's current and future diversity across race and sexuality in mind, I went searching. I inquired of all the nation's Presbyteries, leading scholars in church diversity, and a national network of personal contacts. Given the possibilities for diversity, I sought PC(USA) churches that manifest *both* 20 percent or more of their membership of a different race than the majority *and* 20 percent or more members who are LGBTQ.

The PC(USA)'s "research and development" initiative to establish new, nontraditional congregations, called New Worshipping Communities, has chartered a number of start-up congregations reflecting intersectional viewpoints and values. But, as for established PC(USA) congregations reflecting both thresholds of 20 percent and with longer track records of learning, I could find ten out of about 9,900. I wrote to the pastors of those flocks and asked them to tell me more about their lives together.

MEET SOME OF AMERICA'S MOST DIVERSE AND DYNAMIC CHURCHES

As the responses came in, my sense of pastoral and congregational solitude faded. I rejoiced as one coming out of a wilderness of isolation. One by one, pastors introduced themselves and the inspiring stories of their congregations. These churches manifest all kinds and mixes—large and small; rich, poor, and in-between; barely hanging on and financially comfortable. They are white, Black, and brown; gay, straight, and queer; staunchly Presbyterian and just barely Presbyterian.

All are urban or suburban. All have seen their neighborhoods and cities change. All center their missional identities on radical welcome and social justice. All lean into their own versions of the gift of diversity God has granted them, even though each has its own distinct mix of God's children in the pews. All seek to deepen their diversity, not content with the status quo. Each shows special compassion for "the other" and tries, in its own ways, to place the marginalized and outcast at the center.

In Pittsburgh, East Liberty Presbyterian's grand Gothic structure, funded by the Mellon family in the 1930s, symbolizes the wealth that flowed from its city's once-soaring industrial economy. Since then the neighborhood has sunk low, bringing new socioeconomic realities and opportunities for ministry, and is now recovering again. East Liberty today embraces an identity as the "Cathedral of Hope" for its voice for justice, its wide welcome, and its invitation to the hurting and wounded.

Just off Washington, DC's busy Dupont Circle, the Church of the Pilgrims was chartered in 1902 by the Southern arm of the Presbyterian church as a place for Southern

Presbyterians to worship in what was then a "Northern" presbytery. As with so many, its life followed the upward curve of Presbyterianism, growing steadily through the first half of the twentieth century then experiencing sustained decline in membership and vitality through the second half. As its neighborhood and city manifested different needs and cries for help, Church of the Pilgrims devoted itself to urban ministry and emerged as an early leader in offering inclusive welcome, far different from its roots as a "safe haven" for traditional Southern Presbyterians visiting Washington. In 2016, Ashley Goff, then the associate pastor who responded to my inquiry, described it this way:

> The Southern church was loyal to the ways of white supremacy, embracing slavery and segregation. We have this mixed past of being a place of welcome for young, white Southerners, then a switch to social justice in the 1960s. Now everything is directed to being a place where rainbows fly and #BlackLivesMatter.

In Brooklyn, New York, First Presbyterian's handsome brownstone architecture reflects its origins in wealth. The look of the elegant, dark-wood sanctuary has escaped change over time, but the congregation has shifted from being a once all-white flock to a diverse and missionally engaged congregation. Rev. Adriene Thorne, an African American ballet dancer–turned–pastor, leads her troupe as they chassé and pirouette through having hard conversations, seeking social justice, speaking truth to power, and loving inclusively.

Detroit's Jefferson Avenue Presbyterian sits on the edge of what was once one of the city's finest neighborhoods, where brewing, manufacturing, and automobile magnates built handsome homes with servants' quarters and lovely gardens. Decades later, as its city declined, so did its membership. Rev. Ken Kaibel, the pastor at the time of my initial research, put it plainly when he wrote back in my questionnaire: "We went through a period of death beginning in the 1950s." Then, he recalled the church "began a period of creative experimentation in worship alongside a fearless commitment to social justice."

The PC(USA) was only beginning its forty-year debate over homosexuality when Jefferson Avenue began welcoming LGBTQ people and standing up for their equality in the 1970s and 1980s. A few years ago, members took an electric saw to the decades-old lock mechanism of its grand front doors, whose key was long lost. It was Palm Sunday when the front door of the church swung open, welcoming Jefferson Avenue more widely—literally and figuratively—to a new Detroit. Rev. Matthew Nickel, a fifth-generation Detroiter, finds himself officiating more funerals these days as many of his older members die. Replacing them is a more diverse membership base and the congregation is talking more openly and honestly about topics like white privilege as it enters a new future in a radically changed city.

Capitol Heights Presbyterian was chartered in Denver, Colorado, in 1911. After decades of life as a traditional congregation, it also opened its arms to outsiders, ahead of most churches in the city. In 1985, it voted to serve as sanctuary to those fleeing persecution in Central America. In 1990, it became a "More Light" Church, aligning with one of two national organizations advocating for full LGBTQ inclusion in the PC(USA). Today they hold to a Statement of Faith that reads in part, "I need a community whose goal is to live God's dream of a new creation, empowered by the Spirit of God, whose nurture makes us more than the sum of our parts and empowers us to live as brothers and sisters."

Another early exemplar of diversity and intersectional living is Atlanta's Oakhurst Presbyterian Church. Its once white, middle-class neighborhood shifted to become more African American in the middle of the twentieth century. To be more welcoming and to reflect more accurately what Christ actually looked like, Oakhurst darkened the complexion of the "white" Jesus in its central stained-glass window, attracting criticism and hatred. Under the longtime leadership of Rev. Nibs Stroupe and Caroline Leach, Oakhurst courageously pioneered the hard work of justice-oriented witness and missional identity. Rev. Amantha Barbee, a gifted singer and preacher who is known to mix the two, followed Stroupe in 2019. She leads Oakhurst as the neighborhood deals with gentrification and as Atlanta lives into its fully multicultural future.

Alongside some of the city's finest row houses, Baltimore's Brown Memorial Park Avenue Presbyterian Church was founded in 1869 and built with an investment banking fortune. But Brown Memorial's wealth did not equate to comfortable complacency. In 1963, Brown's pastor and several church members were arrested during the forced desegregation of Gwynn Oak Park. The actions of the church didn't surprise anyone who knew it. A decade earlier, the church founded the second racially integrated nursery school program in the city. When an amicable split moved part of the congregation to the city's northern suburbs, a portion remained, "precisely in the midst of racial and class division, fear and decline. God's call would be sufficient. Listening for God's call, especially in the midst of challenge, continues to shape our life together as community."[10] Today, under the leadership of Rev. Andrew Foster Connors, Brown offers a community center, plays a key role in Baltimore's community organizing movement, and enjoys its historic relationships with Baltimore's vibrant Jewish community.[11]

Outside Baltimore, a group of young disciples with a shared vision of church began meeting in a school gymnasium in Laurel, Maryland. They chartered Oaklands Presbyterian in 1966 and started causing holy trouble soon afterward. Its early pastor helped run the Ku Klux Klan out of town. Its next pastor was a closeted gay man, a secret the church kept. Members protested the Vietnam war and, later, supported their pastor's decision to officiate a same-gender wedding long, long before denominational polity approved. On its fiftieth anniversary in 2016, Rev. LeAnn Hodges pledged Oaklands Presbyterian will continue the work of its founding members as "a safe place to have hard conversations."[12]

Durham Presbyterian Church in Durham, North Carolina, was formed in 2012 when a handful of people from two dying Presbyterian congregations felt called to create a new model for church. They were not motivated by institutional survival. In fact, says Rev. Franklin Golden, "most people there at the beginning left soon after the church was formed because of all that had to die for something new to be born."

The creation of Durham Presbyterian was anchored in one thing: the desire for intimacy across racial and social boundaries. That meant the establishment and maintenance of a covenant relationship with a Hispanic congregation. Says Golden, "We share a building, worship together, partner on ministries where our sister congregation Iglesia Emanuel takes the lead, and seek to draw closer and closer."

Today, Durham Presbyterian is navigating its own uniquely diverse make-up as it focuses outward in its community. Every day, Golden says, the church is reminded of who is really in charge.

"Our efforts at planning, looking ahead, and casting vision reveal how little rides on our understanding or ability. But God has been good to us in giving us one another and helping us learn to love. What we've received is lovelier than what we imagined," Golden reflects.

While it did not surface in my original research, a congregation that stands alongside these forerunners in diversity and intersectional ministry is McKinley Memorial Presbyterian Church, founded in 1912 in Urbana-Champaign, Illinois. As told in Assata Zerai's *Intersectionality in Intentional Communities*, its story is that of "cohesion and contestation in a Presbyterian college-town congregation that was, in the 1940s, largely a heteronormative white, Republican, highly educated, middle-class congregation, which over a forty-year period became" a pioneering blend of members of differing races, sexual identities, and classes with a deep commitment to social justice. McKinley members, Zerai writes, "have struggled within their own walls, within their presbytery, in the denomination at large, and in university and residential communities to supplant traditional gender hierarchies, make marriage accessible to all, and intentionally address issues of racism."[13]

Resurrection reigns in all of these congregations—and, in many, courage comes from near-death experiences. A palpable joy, energy, and enthusiasm flow from members' commitment to the hard work of sustaining their mission, witness, and viability. Worship in these places is fluid, flexible and vibrant. Polity and leadership structures are adapted to be truly representative and, where needed, to rebalance power and privilege in leadership. Scars from hurts, whether from life's battles or internal church conflict, are not hidden but shown vulnerably for the sake of healing and learning. When it comes to community, members turn outward as much or more than inward. They practice evangelism by publicly bearing witness to God's love and justice.

Pastors at these places understand that, as with their congregations, they have turned down a side road away from what goes for church in many places. They don't dream of multisite churches. High production quality videos don't appear mid-worship on giant screens next to thirty-foot-high speaker stacks. Worship leadership reflects the array of diversity in the pews. Life together at these churches is messy and magnificent; gutsy and glorious; unpredictable, unpretentious, and upside down from the norm.

"Because of the commitment to radical welcome, over time, we have attracted people from all walks of life, many of whom have found themselves at some point on the outside looking in," says Rev. Hodges at Oaklands Presbyterian in Maryland. "What seems to unify the congregation is a shared sense of knowing how precious it is to be celebrated when that is not always the norm."

LIBERATION AND NEW PERSPECTIVE

What do these congregations have in common? In what ways did their near-death experiences prepare them for what God would do with them? As God showed with Jesus and his followers, a brush with the tomb can have powerful transformative effects. Each of these churches gained a new perspective, one liberated from the old, inward-focused, risk-averse ways that marked the mainline Protestant church throughout the first half of the twentieth century when these and so many other churches rode the close alignment of Christianity and American culture.

As they emerged from their wilderness periods, however, each began to live out of a new understanding of how God could use their material assets. Each brought new understanding of how to practice evangelism to those on the margins—and how to value and learn from those newcomers coming in from the outside. Each congregation was stirred to new, but not always easy and comfortable, life as faith communities that put justice at the center of everything they do. Long before the idea of intersectionality would be conceived, these congregations prepared a way for God to do a new thing.

Today, even as they have been re-formed, none of these congregations would say they "have it made." But all would say their faith has never been more alive as they seek to answer God's call to stand in the gap for others.

Their experiences informed our new journey at Caldwell. Having found our peers, the people of Caldwell and I now had a broader context for what God was doing with us and how to try to be the best stewards of the unfathomable "Miracle on Fifth Street" that had occurred before our very eyes.

THE CHURCH
OF BOTH/AND

So much of what seems to be broken in America stems from the temptation to cling to "either/or" certainty in a time of "both/and" truths.

Whether our affinity is with class, race, sexual orientation, or even our neighborhood or civic organization, the instincts God gave us for survival by affiliating only with our own have an ugly and persistent side. In Christ, God calls us to transcend these instincts and strive for the beloved community. And so do other voices. Shelves of studies show the benefits of diversity are manifold and irrefutable—in education, in organizational dynamics, and in the marketplace, perhaps America's favorite measuring stick.

Decades ago, when I wrote speeches for Bank of America (first North Carolina National Bank and subsequently NationsBank) chief executive officer Hugh McColl, he made commitment to diversity a staple of his leadership philosophy. In the early 1990s, it guided him to launch groundbreaking work-life balance programs for working parents so they could pursue their careers and have a family. He set high goals for hiring African Americans at all levels of the company and for doing business with women- and minority-owned businesses because that made the company better. Mr. McColl didn't believe in just saying the "right things" in speeches and media interviews. He led by a simple creed: if the company took care of its associates, they would take care of their customers and that would take care of the shareholders.

In the heady years of banking consolidation, the company bought and merged with bank after bank after bank as it created the country's first coast-to-coast giant. In my years there, it grew from $60 billion in assets in 1990 to $2.5 trillion in 2008. As thousands of new team members joined the company each year, Mr. McColl's message was clear and consistent: he expected—and rewarded—diversity, equality, and respect for multiple perspectives. With every acquisition of another bank, Mr. McColl met with its leaders. The train was leaving the station, he told them, and people not on board with these values would be left on the platform.

This is not to say the church should mimic the private sector. The goals of businesses and the work of the gospel differ vastly. Still, data show time and again how diverse organizations of all types are more effective, including churches. With the unatoned weight of America's original sin of slavery still draped from our neck, plus a long history of subordinating women and a range of oppressed groups of people, we as a nation have been slow and halting to adopt what Mr. McColl understood and practiced.

Over the last century and a half, social scientists, scholars, activists, prophets, and others have shined a light on how different minority subsets of the populace suffer their own particular oppressions and challenges. Research and thought leadership focused on white women, and then African Americans and other people of color. The effect of poverty and class was added to the scholarship and analysis along with inequalities rooted in disability and, most recently, the hate, prejudice, and discrimination shown to the LGBTQ community across all colors of its rainbow. For decades, activists and others brought the inequities and inequalities for these and other marginalized people to light. But these areas of study and analysis mostly occurred in distinct lanes that never crossed.

That single-lane thinking changed in important ways when feminist thought was applied to issues of race. Ida B. Wells, bell hooks, and others advanced thinking about how identities and their respective forms of oppression interact in dynamic ways. The idea of intersectionality deepens that understanding. More an analytical tool than a scholarly discipline, intersectionality helps us see the dynamics of multiple types of diversity as they converge in one community or institution. Intersectionality promotes justice in how it analyzes and challenges the ways different forms of inequality and inequity overlap and compound.

In their book *Intersectionality*, Patricia Hill Collins and Sirma Bilge cite Kimberlé Crenshaw's 1991 *Stanford Law Review* article, "Mapping the Margins: Intersectionality, Identity Politics, and Violence against Women of Color,"[1] as the origin of the term and idea of intersectionality. Emanating from Black feminism, this framework updated the development of race, class, and gender studies by highlighting the limitations of separate and distinct approaches to understanding the experience of minority groups.

Collins and Bilge argue that, as a tool for any organization, system, or institution, intersectional analysis works best through both *critical inquiry* and *critical praxis*. In other words, we must assess the facts and then work toward justice and equality based on our analysis.

The idea of intersectionality moved closer to center stage in the first days of the Trump administration as millions of shocked voters protested the election outcome in cities nationwide.[2] The media's hasty label of these as "women's marches" immediately proved too narrow and drew criticism. Joining the white women in raising their concerns about President Trump's views of women were a range of allies—supportive men, yes, but also Black and brown people, immigrants and refugees, members of the LGBTQ community, children, and more, each with grave concerns about the new president's stated views.

One week later, Trump's presidential executive order banning entrance into the US from seven Muslim-majority nations sparked similar protests with the same kind of intersectionality, a convergence of minority, marginalized populations.

Suddenly, mainstream media pundits and commentators added the term *intersectional* to their vocabulary as they described these gatherings of mutual support, empathy, and shared concern. After years as an obscure idea known to few, the idea of intersectionality entered the mainstream.

As quickly, critics of intersectional analysis rushed into the conversation. To them, intersectionality only aggravates existing divisions and fissures in American culture. As a message of so-called "identity politics," critics said, it undercut the notion of a purported, "pull-yourselves-up-by-your-bootstraps" meritocracy that sees beyond color, class, sexuality or other difference. In politics and other realms, conservative commentators bashed intersectionality as an "ideology" and even a "religion."

To be sure, intersectionality does "trouble the waters," as the old hymn says. It complicates the status quo of virtually any US institution or system, given the long reign of white, male, hetero supremacy. If applied bluntly and dogmatically, the idea of intersectionality can aggravate existing divisions. However, intersectionality need not embrace any ideology or party politics. Rather, it can enable an honest, critical examination of how close—or how far—America is from its promised goal of equality for all.

CONFESSIONS OF A SINGLE-AXIS THINKER

Given the projected demographic future of our country and the hopeful possibilities of a more diverse populace, we could all use a set of intersectional lenses. I'm still working on mine. I like to think I escaped my Southern roots without deep prejudice. Instead, I developed what Grace Ji-Sun Kim and Susan Shaw call "single-axis thinking."

With a father as a newspaper reporter, columnist, and editor, and a mother as an educator, centrist-to-progressive ideals were part of our household. But so was independent thinking and intellectual rigor. My father, Reese Cleghorn, covered the civil rights movement as a journalist and opinion writer in the 1950s and 1960s. He interviewed and came to work with its giants, including Rev. Dr. Martin Luther King Jr., John Lewis, Julian Bond, Andrew Young, and many others. Progressives on the forefront of the civil rights movement came to our home for Saturday night dinners and dialogues, though the closest I got as a young boy was to try to listen under the hallway door threshold. In 1967, my father stepped away from daily journalism and into the movement itself. He joined the Southern Regional Council, producing a range of publications that fueled the movement and cowriting with Pat Watters a history of the Student

Nonviolent Coordinating Committee's pivotal role in the civil rights movement, *Climbing Jacob's Ladder*.

In these ways, I was blessed to be around a range of forward thinkers as a kid. In those and the following years, I attended an elite independent school, chiefly because my mother, Gwen Cleghorn, taught there, providing a break on tuition. Our family was closer to middle class, but the sons and daughters of Atlanta's scions were my classmates and friends. After my parents' divorce, I saw the struggle of my single mother in a demanding, professional role with only modest income. This was in the 1970s, before many employers gave thought to what single parents faced.

My upbringing, then, was a mix of ideas and values with a mostly progressive slant. Nonetheless, I was inevitably developing the blindness that came with the privileges of my race, gender, class, and social capital.

In college, that blindness worsened. I enrolled at Washington and Lee University because of its small-college feel and reputation for excellence in journalism education. I received a great education. But it was inescapably limiting as an all-male school (the board voted for coeducation weeks after I graduated in 1984) and as an institution steeped in the identity of the general who led the Confederate army (and, after Appomattox, served for four years as the university president). Washington and Lee now annually ranks as one of top liberal arts universities in the nation. It educated me well in many areas, including journalism and the liberal arts. But, along the way, my blinders of privilege grew worse.

Fortunately, God was not through schooling me. As I gained a little life experience and maturity, I became a different kind of student of history. I've spent the last thirty years unpacking and extending the genealogical research my patrician grandmother painstakingly gathered in spiral-bound notebooks. Through this full genealogy (which I have in depth because of my skin color and privilege), history came alive as I followed my family's story through seven generations of US history.

With that history comes the truth of how my family, as with so many, benefited from white supremacy at the cost of others. It started around 1735, when a young William Cleghorn landed from Scotland. He became the progenitor of thousands of Cleghorns in America, most across the South.

He came with little, most likely because his older brothers took their shares of whatever inheritance there was before he got his turn. After arriving in America, he married (coincidentally in the same county where I went to college in Virginia) and settled on some land outside what is now Rutherfordton, North Carolina. He took up farming and documents show he owned enslaved Africans.

The next generation eventually settled in northeast Georgia, around today's Rome, in what was then the Cherokee nation. My great-great-grandfather was appointed by the governor of Georgia to serve as an agent to the Cherokees, who were being removed under the direction of President Andrew Jackson. Records of his six-month stint as agent to the Cherokees are sparse but yield one letter by him. He wrote to notify the governor that a small number of Cherokees had remained in the area after most were swept westward in the tragic Trail of Tears. In the letter, he suggested to the governor that those families be left alone, but there is no further correspondence to reveal the outcome.

Two Cleghorn brothers, William and my great-grandfather, John, left their home as young men to serve in the Confederate army. A third brother, Cicero, remained at home and ran a manufacturing operation. John served as a quartermaster in the Western theater with the Army of Tennessee. Documents show he ordered shoes and supplies for the troops from his brother at home, Cicero. That means my family, for a time, was enriched by the "Cause." William fought in the infantry under Gen. Robert E. Lee in the Eastern theater until he died on May 5, 1864, in the Battle of the Wilderness, north of Richmond. Eleven months later, his brother John and the remnant of the rebel army were on their way to meet Gen. Joseph Johnston in North Carolina for one last stand when Lee surrendered. Because they served in different theaters of the war, either John or William Cleghorn was in virtually every major battle in the Civil War.

I've studied these truths not to glorify the cause but to face what they represent. I can walk almost any Civil War battlefield and identify where my ancestors fought and, in some cases, died for a system and a way of life that is utterly foreign and repugnant to me. A few years ago, out of the blue, a distant cousin introduced himself and gifted me some of the letters John and William Cleghorn wrote to their relatives at home during the war. They described the army's movements and the soldiers' conditions. The brothers inquired about their friends at home and even asked to be remembered to "the darkies," those they enslaved (as if the enslaved people could forget!).

After Lee's surrender, Capt. John Cleghorn returned to Summerville, Georgia. He married, built a fine, Victorian home that overlooked the town and took up business as a merchant. His life there took on several tragic turns. His daughter was murdered at the foot of their driveway in a love triangle gone bad. What money the family had was lost when someone defrauded a bank that John Cleghorn had started, no doubt in part capitalizing on his reputation as

Capt. Cleghorn. The big home was passed on to my grandfather, but he died a short time later. His wife, Nona Martin Cleghorn, saw one child die as an infant and another live until sixteen before he died of birth defects, leaving the family name only to my father. As a single mother, she took on renters in the big Victorian home until it burned in the 1960s. She lived out her days in a rented apartment as a town matriarch with little money but all the privilege of her lineage.

My father seized whatever education he could get locally and then boarded the train for Emory University in Atlanta at age sixteen. After graduating, he entered journalism, covered and advanced the emergence of a so-called "New South" that, in many ways, has yet to be as new as he had hoped.

What does one make of such a family history, stained by complicity in the forced removal of the Cherokee people, and generations of owning slaves? I have done my best to research, understand it, and own its fullness as much as I can. I have tried to learn from it. I have taught it to my daughters and confessed its truth to my congregation and during other talks and presentations. I have tried to understand its privilege, pain, and, in some cases, tragic consequences.

No matter how hard I study the ground of the Civil War battlefields I've walked, I cannot discern the thinking or motivations of the Cleghorn brothers who fought there. But here is the truth that can be discerned, one that shouldn't be sugarcoated. My ancestors participated in the removal of American Indians from land that was theirs. They fought, and some died, to maintain a system that is still the scourge of our nation. The Union may have won the Civil War for the emancipation of African Americans stolen from their own native land, but the United States has ever since relied on the forced labor and subjugation of African Americans to function.

So, I must ask myself: How am I complicit today in continuing the legacies of "America's original sin" or in fostering any other structures or institutions that undermine the nation's promise of justice and equality? What battlefields are we called to march to end slavery's insidious effects of white supremacy? How will history judge the four score or so years I will have on this earth? How can I still be freed from the chains of my privilege and the blindness of my myopia? How can the church and the nation regain our sight?

The cry of the prophet Isaiah still echoes:

Shout out, do not hold back!
    Lift up your voice like a trumpet!
Announce to my people their rebellion,
    to the house of Jacob their sins.
Yet day after day they seek me
    and delight to know my ways,
as if they were a nation that practiced righteousness
    and did not forsake the ordinance of their God;
they ask of me righteous judgments,
    they delight to draw near to God.
"Why do we fast, but you do not see?
    Why humble ourselves, but you do not notice?"
Look, you serve your own interest on your fast-day,
    and oppress all your workers. . . .
Is not this the fast that I choose:
    to loose the bonds of injustice,
to undo the thongs of the yoke,
    to let the oppressed go free,
and to break every yoke? (Isa 58:1–3, 6)

58

WHY INTERSECTIONALITY?

All of that brings us to the question: Why intersectionality as one critical lens for people like me and for a nation whose moral balance sheet doesn't balance?

Because it offers to help level the playing field. Because it creates a more just nation and heals our blind spots and prejudices. Because it opens our eyes to the truth of others' lives as shaped not just by racism but also by sexism, homophobia, classism, and all the other "-isms" that we impose to divide the family of God and protect our tribes. Because it helps us find commonalities with others that are deeper than what we see "on the surface."

Intersectional analysis requires that I acknowledge how deeply I am formed by my "native" experience in the white, upper-middle class of America, including how that background can limit my ministry. It requires me to muster all the humility and self-awareness I can. It means I can't stop pressing for deeper understanding and empathy. It calls me to check my privilege where I should and to use my voice where I can to point to the voices of those too long silenced or shouted down.

Some may say I should just step aside. They may say I am an inappropriate champion of intersectional analysis, that I should be silent and let the long-silenced speak for themselves. They may say that championing this perspective is not my fight to fight or my story to tell. I understand and respect those opinions. At the same time, in all of my frailties and failures, inadequacies and imperfections, I feel compelled to bear witness to how my field of vision is broadened through an intersectional analysis of all that is around me.

Then, we ask: Why intersectionality *in the church*?

Because the church has lost the confidence and respect of

multiple generations of Americans. Ongoing financial and sexual scandals. Homophobia and hypocrisy. Judgment-laden preaching. The incestuous alignment of the evangelical movement with the values of Trump's America. All of these have alienated generations of Americans from the church.

An August 2019 poll by the *Wall Street Journal* and NBC News found the percentage of Americans who say religion or belief in God is very important to them has fallen by one-third over the last two decades, from 62 percent to 48 percent. Only 30 percent of Americans aged eighteen to thirty-eight, by far the most diverse generation and the one that will shape what organized religion looks like in the future, said religion is very important to them.[3]

Why should the church broaden its view and invitation? Some assert the "market case" of pure pragmatism. In her work, *Intersectionality in Intentional Communities*, Assata Zerai describes the church's decline in both public confidence and in numerical attendance. "One important potential source of new members in mainstream churches is expansion from predominantly white middle class or working class populations as they embrace greater levels of demographic diversity and inclusion."[4] In light of America's "new" identity, she adds, "Progress toward multicultural society requires successful multicultural, multiracial, integrated organizations that are not ordered solely by class, gender, sexuality, or other dominant social categories."[5]

To be sure, following Christ is not about interpreting poll data, building a business case, managing risk for optimal returns, or following a marketing strategy. Instead, as Zerai adds, intersectional church is about liberation—of those who are captive to their own hatred, bigotry, blindness, prejudice, and the systems that sustain those values. But not just those people. The intersectional church is also providing sight to those of us with so many blind spots, known and unknown to us, that one day we may sing, "And now I see."

"In fact," write Grace Ji-Sun Kim and Susan M. Shaw in *Intersectional Theology: An Introductory Guide*, "the embrace of intersectional thinking by dominant groups is absolutely essential to progress for us all because dominant groups hold the social, economic, political, and religious power to make significant change."[6]

What, then, is intersectional *theology*? First, it recognizes how men in positions of power and influence, mostly white or otherwise in the majority, have been the primary shapers of theology for eons. That means the church and its seminaries privileged these white, Eurocentric voices over others that have been subdued. But those suppressed voices have much to say and teach to those of us with privilege about what marginalization looks and feels like. Intersectional theology invites us who have been in the center to leave our safe zones, travel out to the margins, see the world from that perspective, invite the once-edged-out into the center, and prioritize their ideas and voices.

That is *not* to say the voices of traditional power and influence need to be silenced altogether. That would commit just another form of what Kim and Shaw call "single-axis," either/or thinking. It is to say we need to privilege voices other than the majority in order to live into God's hope and vision of an equal and beloved community. That is "both/and" thinking.

"The recognition that there are multiple axes of thinking widens our scope of critical reflection, learning, and theological reflection. If we fall into single-axis thinking, we flatten our diversity within our group and ignore the myriad ways intersecting oppressions shape experience," Kim and

Shaw write. "Both/and thinking requires we imagine the subjects of our theologizing in all of their complexity."[7]

Theologically, this invitation to imagine God's people and God's stories "in all of their complexity" requires many of us to loosen our moorings, inasmuch as they limit us, to the "giants" that shaped our tradition and theological formation. Calvin, Luther, Barth, Bonhoeffer, and other white male voices gave us the Reformed tradition, winning countless disciples' hearts, minds, souls, and strength. Now we are invited, if not required, to hold them up alongside past, current, and emerging minority voices.

What, then, does the church of both/and look like? The church of both/and invites perspectives that don't replace, but do sometimes challenge and disturb the ways so many have read God's stories for so long. It awakens us to empathize with the immigrants who are fleeing for their lives to find opportunity and new life here.

The church of both/and stirs us to hear Christ's instruction to embrace the little children—not so we can hug our own kids more tightly and provide only for them, but to be troubled by the truth that, because of racial disparities in education tools and resources, African American students often lag behind national educational score averages and will be pushed back even further as the COVID-19 pandemic accentuates the digital divide.

The church of both/and analyzes housing, who owns homes and who doesn't, to understand how and why today's racially imbalanced patterns of home ownership happened. It lifts up the cries of the Old Testament prophet Habakkuk, "Woe to him who builds his realm by unjust gain, to set his nest on high, to escape the clutches of the ruin."[8]

The church of both/and invites us to righteous anger that

Black and Latinx families in places like Charlotte spend 57 percent of their household income on housing, twice the target for all families.

The church of both/and offers not just tolerance but love, dignity, empowerment, and full embrace, in the pews and in leadership, of all of God's noncisgender and/or nonheterosexual children as it brings to life Isaiah's words, "For this is what the Lord says: 'To the eunuchs who keep my Sabbaths, who choose what pleases me and hold fast to my covenant—to them I will give within my temple and its walls a memorial and a name better than sons and daughters.'"

The church of both/and creates safe places for those who struggle with mental health, greeting them with the words of Psalm 57:1:

Be merciful to me, O God, be merciful to me,
    for in you my soul takes refuge;
in the shadow of your wings I will take refuge,
    until the destroying storms pass by.

MORE THAN JUST PREACHING

The both/and intersectional church is more than thinking theologically. It is *acting* theologically. Case and Shaw write, and Caldwell Presbyterian's experience affirms, that intersectional theology as a lens for critical analysis necessarily leads to action. It recognizes power can take many forms— "power-over," "power-with," and also "power-to,"—the agency to act according to Christ's radical (meaning original) teaching.[9] Intersectionality opens "space for dialogue and embracing the other, which is needed in a world torn apart by fear and religious tensions."[10]

It provides opportunities for change-making coalitions

that go beyond people of difference just sitting beside each other in the pews; that intersect the interests of different minority groups with those in the majority, ideally centering the voices of those who have traditionally been ignored or shouted down; that leverage the church and its resources by joining with neighborhood, nonprofit, and public resources. These coalitions, within and beyond the faith community, can remove the buoys that float on the top of the water and keep us in our separate swim lanes as we pursue justice.

An intersectional viewpoint sparks a new understanding of ecclesiology and leadership development that elevates voices long marginalized. It challenges church polity where it has fallen behind. At Caldwell, for example, when the session re-formed after the 2006–2007 resurrection, we knew we had to blend the old senior saints with a representative mix of the newcomers. That meant taking "holy risks," like ordaining elders who were LGBTQ before PC(USA) polity allowed it.

Ultimately, Kim and Shaw assert an intersectional church is also, by nature, a "resistant church" that challenges political, financial, social, and other constructs that protect inequality and work against God's call for a just and fair covenant community:

On the whole, the church's history is primarily one of collusion with dominating powers. Of course, across this history are scattered examples of a counter-church, a church resisting the dominating powers of racism, misogyny, transphobia, ableism, capitalism, homophobia, xenophobia, colonialism, and ageism. Intersectionality calls the church to be the resistant church. With an awareness of intersecting identities and interlocking systems of oppression, the church

64

must resist the organization of structures of power that maintain the dominance of the elite. Following the example of Jesus, the church must stand against worldly powers that force the poor and vulnerable and marginalized into ever-more constrained spaces, seeking their invisibility and, ultimately, their destruction.[11]

The intersectional church of both/and sees the other, in all of their forms, in the Scriptures. It considers the plight of those who are othered in light of Christ's call to loving inclusion. It reflects on its participation with or opposition to ways the other is harmed. It acts to effect equality.

"DID HE REALLY GO THERE?"

Destiny and Trené are a lesbian couple and two of the loveliest souls and most devoted disciples one will ever meet. They grew up not that far apart but not knowing each other, both in Baptist churches in rural South Carolina and solidly in the African American tradition, loving Jesus and the communities of faith that raised and sustained them. Later, they met at a historically Black college and felt a spark. Years later, they could no longer keep how God made them a public secret, so they chose to be wed and live joyfully as who they are. They found Caldwell as their church home, driving thirty minutes to get to church but rarely missing a Sunday and getting deeply involved in the church's activities and ministries.

When we met to begin planning their wedding, they recalled a sermon from one of their first Sundays as visitors to Caldwell. They were looking for a church that preached the gospel and accepted them fully. In that sermon, as they recalled it, I discussed racial reconciliation and race relations. As I have a few times over the decade, as they recalled, I spoke about how I'd wrestled with my family's history and how we all shared a call to the ongoing work of joining God in letting "justice roll down like waters and righteousness like an ever-flowing stream." They remember they first gave me a long look, a straight, white, white-haired preacher with a notable Georgia accent robed in a stole and a cross.

Then they looked at each other with wide eyes.

"Did he just say that? Is he really going there?" Destiny had whispered to Trené.

"I guess he is!" Trené had whispered back. And they'd settled back in their seats to see what may happen next at their new, odd, and unpredictable church home.

My point is not whatever I said that day was life changing to anyone in the pews. It is to say God desires for us all to tell the truth about ourselves, our pasts, and our blind spots, as well as our hopes and dreams to live more deeply into God's purposes for truth and justice.

By God's hand, this change continues at Caldwell as other voices are heard. Sasha, a vice president at a Charlotte bank with global responsibilities, took the pulpit and brought tears to our eyes as she told of the journey she traversed while she made her transition, including fearing how her own family members might harm her. Abong, a seminary graduate and social worker, shares with the congregation the plight of her native Cameroon, Africa. Curious visitors, mostly white and cisgender, come and see what God is doing. Some don't return. Others join the church, sensing their own call to learn and grow in the faith in new ways in our setting.

What also continues at Caldwell are all the routine things in church life. Young couples bring their babies to be baptized. The last of the original Caldwell remnant are now living out their final days. The finance committee works to balance the budget. Volunteers faithfully teach our children. The church administrator wonders what will break or fail next on our almost-century-old campus.

Life in church.

The gospel, ancient and ever new. The same, but different.

Both/and.

CENTERING "OTHERED" VIEWS OF SCRIPTURE

One of the reasons I love ministry is the Holy Bible, God's inspired and written word, isn't so much infallible as it is inexhaustible. We can study it for the rest of our lives and it will never fail to say something new—if we are receptive. In this age when we automatically follow whatever directions our smartphone map apps give us, we stick to familiar roads and routes. We become blind to the alternative byways that can lead us to discover what God is saying now. We stay in our lanes, guided by the same, "traditional" interpretations of Scripture, not knowing how we are limiting ourselves and our understanding of God. After all, as Jacob discovered on the road back to Canaan and as the apostle Paul found on the road to Damascus, God may just be waiting for us around the corner to show us something new.

With that in mind, this chapter invites us to take a road that, for many of us, will be the one "less traveled." We will practice hearing others' voices, whoever we are. This chapter summons the theologian that lives within each of us. In sermons and Sunday school lessons, books and even movies, most of us have experienced Scripture as interpreted by a narrow band of perspectives. That puts us on dangerous ground if we seek to share God's word, love, and justice with the emerging America, if we ever hope to reverse Americans' plummeting view of religion as a core value. Just as we raise our children to learn multiple languages for today's and tomorrow's pluralistic world, we need to become more "multilingual" in hearing Scripture.

This chapter invites us to hear with new ears what Paul may mean in his letter to the Galatians, with a focus on Galatians 3:27–28. I know plenty of folks who would quickly decline the chance to go with Paul as tour guide for such a journey. Some progressive Christians may turn up their nose at the very mention of the apostle's name, given how some of his words have been used to defend racism, clobber LGBTQ people, and keep women in the kitchen and the bedroom. Others find Paul impenetrable, full stop. I get that and respectfully ask for reconsideration.

As one raised by parents who taught me to love words and language, my first interest in Paul was for his lyrical writing—at times poetic, other times subtly humorous, and always multilayered in depth. Paul was also as a man for his time—and ours. He found the capacity to step outside of himself and his native experience to cross differences of all kinds and relay the gospel to all of God's children.

Born to privilege as a Roman citizen who later became a powerful Pharisee, he began as a zealot driven by his absolute certainty of what he knew to be "true" about God. That left little room for other ideas. He stuck to the main roads, in other words. But God found him anyway. In a vision of Jesus, Paul said, God spun him around and rerouted him. Funny how Jesus does that.

From Paul's old ways of "single-axis" thinking he was born again to a new perspective and empathy shaped by "multiaxis thinking." After the incident on the road to Damascus, Paul traveled thousands of miles of backroads, seeking first-century intersections of cultures, religions, politics, power, gender, and class. His new people became those fearless followers of the Jesus movement, many he had earlier relished in persecuting and murdering. For his trouble, his faith, and his witness, he would be murdered by the defenders of the status quo.

Paul's letters make up about half of the New Testament. These letters include his own, some written as tributes to him, and others written in his name and tradition. He may be best known for the epistle to the Romans, from which vast systematic theologies have been erected. Romans, chapters 8 to 11, have been lifted up and placed alongside John 3:16 as bedrock to Christianity. No seminarian graduates without at least some intensive study of Romans and other Pauline writings.

But just when one thinks they have Paul nailed down, he says some of the most bewildering things. One of the most bewildering comes in his letter to the Galatians. As was often the case with Paul and the churches he started, the saints at Galatia weren't acting very saintly. Conflict (imagine that, in a church!) stirred. A faction of purists was insisting being a true believer in Jesus necessitated Gentiles be circumcised to join the line of Abrahamic Judaism that was Jesus's lineage. If nothing else, it was a statement of commitment! Some of the Galatians wrote to Paul seeking advice. As always, he had a clear and emphatic opinion.

Paul wrote back to speak against the claim by those he called "false apostles." Because of Christ, he said there is not any one physical mark of a Christian, that is, circumcision or anything else the Old Testament law may include. Rather, he wrote, "We know that a person is justified not by works of the law but through faith in Jesus Christ."[1]

Paul implored the Galatians to grasp how God, in Christ, had superseded the law *and* circumcision as the mark of faith. Belief in Christ, Paul insisted, is the common ground where believers of all races, ethnicities, and origins can gather as one. Circumcision with the intent to gain justification in Christ was not only unnecessary, it was heresy that separated its practitioners from Christ, who suffered and died for those who believe in him. *The Message* translation by Eugene H. Peterson picks up on Paul's skill with an occasional pun, noting the physical risk with circumcision: "I suspect you would never intend this, but this is what happens. When you attempt to live by your own religious plans and projects, you are cut off from Christ, you fall out of grace."[2]

Christ came so ethnic and other differences would become subordinate to a true, new identity in the faith, Paul wrote. Individual differences do not disappear or become any less important. They contribute to the rich fabric of unity amid diversity for those who put their Christianity above all else. In Galatians 3:27–28, Paul makes what some may say was his most radical statement of all.

As many of you as were baptized into Christ have clothed yourselves with Christ. There is no longer Jew or Greek, there is no longer slave or free, there is no longer male and female; for all of you are one in Christ Jesus.[3]

What? As Destiny asked Trené when I caught her attention in that sermon about race, "Did he really go there?" Paul, this former poster child of either/or, hierarchical, male-dominated, Christian-slaughtering zealotry? Did he just say Christ overcomes all our differences, power positions, and desperate tribalism in his offer of unity amidst diversity? How do we square Paul's claim with the rest of his writings? How do we understand its first-century context and translate it to today's America, when our differences of race, gender, class, sexual orientation, faith, neighborhood, and more seem poised to tear apart the nation?

For the church, can Paul's claim interest us in the kind of community in Christ that unlocks all of the potential and possibilities of the emerging "new America?"

As an exercise in intersectional theology, this chapter offers needed alternatives to scriptural interpretations by straight, white, dead men. Instead, we privilege others and perhaps catch at least a glimpse of the gospel beyond our blind spots.

For that exercise, we turn to voices far different than those many of us encounter in sermons or Sunday school lessons. These are theologians who are, respectively, African American, feminist, LGBTQ, and, more specifically, LGBTQ of color. Can these voices liberate us from our either/or certainty? Can they help us work on our both/and hearing of the word? Can they entice us to abandon the fast lane of mainline biblical interpretation and explore new paths of how to listen to God?

Come to the intersection of perspectives and sit and listen, not to completely surrender one's familiar hearing of Paul, but to be in dialogue with others.

AN AFRICAN AMERICAN PERSPECTIVE

As a first "minority perspective," we turn to Brad Braxton. Braxton is a scholar and founder of the multicultural Open Church of Maryland in Baltimore and a lecturer at multiple divinity schools. He offers a constructive and instructive example of the search for our identity in Christ in his work, *No Longer Slaves: Galatians and African American Experience.*

He roots his reading of Paul in Galatians in an important understanding—that for African Americans, spirituality is a path to self-love, self-respect, a sense of justice, and equality rooted in divine love. The knowledge that God loves them unconditionally frames Black people's understanding of the limits of any others who may try to wield power over them or place a value on their worth, he stipulates.

Out of this conviction, Braxton interprets Galatians as Paul siding with the marginalized, namely the uncircumcised believers in Christ who were under pressure by the majority to be circumcised to prove their faith.

In Galatians, Paul reports that, at a conference at Antioch, the apostle Peter had flipped his position. After seeming to agree in private that circumcision was not necessary, Peter later refused to eat with the uncircumcised, excluding them and reversing his position in public. Thus, Braxton adds, Peter joined with what could be called the traditional power of the time—the law-fearing Judaizers who insisted on circumcision to connect new believers back to the original patriarch, Abraham.

Braxton has seen this kind of public reversal before, calling it the kind of "playacting"[4] African Americans recognize when white power figures and structures fail to keep their promises to bring about equality and justice.

When Braxton arrives at the pivotal passage of Galatians

74

3:27–28, he notes two points. This passage is not, as some interpreters have said, eschatological. In other words, Paul is not writing only about the end time and the final destiny of the soul, some far and away kingdom of God that is separated from our day-to-day struggles. No, Braxton says, Paul is addressing the urgency of the situation present among the Galatians and Paul's desire for their "present harmony."[5] In that claim, Braxton states, we can hear Paul speaking to our own present situation as well.

As important, Braxton also claims Galatians 3:27–28 is not meant to erase social distinctions. In other words, to say there is no longer slave or free, Greek or Jew, male and female is not another way of saying God's vision is of a melting pot in which all the ingredients turn into one unappetizing color. Nor is it to be simplified to the fallacious idea of "seeing beyond color."

Instead, it's about fundamental inequality—power and dominance of one group over another. To be in Christ is to be free of tyranny of one group over another, resulting not in a "race-less"[6] society but in one in which unity amid diversity can be realized and brought to life in Christ. Our distinctions and differences matter in constructive ways.

Braxton writes, "Christ has freed the African American to say, 'yes' to blackness."[7]

Our chance at unity and justice in Christ is about spiritual empathy for those who are different rather than the physical mark of circumcision or any other litmus test. Given the pain of Black experiences in America, Braxton notes, Paul would want us to believe Christ would become Black to experience Black suffering. That, Braxton asserts, is the power of the words "in Christ" for Paul.

This is a powerful concept that can spur the white church to work harder to understand Black experiences in

America. Braxton allows for the conclusion of many scholars that Paul's words in Galatians 3:27–28 about slave/free, Jew/Greek, and male/female touch on three spheres of social strife: ethnic relationships, social class, and gender relationships. Understandably, he connects Paul's call for us to move beyond single-axis thinking primarily to the Black experience.

This kind of laser focus is needed in these days when overt white supremacy has unabashedly stepped out of the shadows. Still, with intersectionality in mind, I may ask Braxton why he did not offer even a few words about whether Paul's radical claim in Galatians 3:27–28 may also illuminate how we understand the experience of other minority and marginalized groups. That would be truly intersectional, but it was not Braxton's purpose at the time he wrote, and I respect that.

Other African American voices do draw a broader circle, however. For instance, in *True to Our Native Land*, editor Brian Blount, president of Union Presbyterian Seminary, includes this brief sidebar to Braxton's Galatians commentary:

> African Americans must ratchet up their study of Paul. The liberative benefits that can be gleaned from his counsel are legion. . . . African American preachers too often use his words as uncritical supports for the less than liberating way in which the church works with women, gays and lesbians, church and state issues, and other matters of grave contemporary consequence.[8]

A FEMINIST PERSPECTIVE

For a feminist interpretation of Galatians, we turn to Brigitte Kahl, professor of New Testament at Union Theological Seminary in New York and author of the commentary chapter called "Galatians: On Discomfort about Gender and Other Problems of Otherness."[9] As with Braxton, Kahl says Paul is siding with the oppressed in the Galatians controversy. She writes Galatians could be considered "one of the foundational sources of Western thinking about and actualizing difference in the form of dominance—by excluding, exploiting, and exterminating the others."[10]

She continues:

> If Galatians is read in this way, Galatians 3:28, one of the most important biblical declarations about the issue of justice among nations, races, classes, and genders, can only be perceived as a kind of isolated spark, thrown off from a liberating, egalitarian practice in the church before and beside Paul in the dark and forbidding context of Galatians.[11]

Almost mournfully, Kahl wonders whether Galatians 3:27–28 could reveal, for a momentary flash, the "authentic" Paul, one who was later silenced by editors in Rome and reinterpreted by Martin Luther, Augustine, and others in ways that muted his radical side.

As for Galatians' focus on circumcision, Kahl also explores Galatians as a "letter targeting maleness"[12] and related to issues of masculinity. For Paul, the very gospel was at stake when the pro-circumcision group moved to use its vested power over the uncircumcised. To do so, Kahl writes, was to advance a false gospel given the "inclusive Judaism made possible in and by Christ."[13]

For Kahl, this oppression reflects the contemporary separation of the privileged and the underprivileged and, for that matter, any other instance when the gospel is used as a wedge to define one over the other. So, Kahl states, "it is no accident" that Paul takes this chance to offer his first extensive statement on justification in Christ. Justification, as Kahl interprets Paul, enables "the other to be the other," a theology not of oppression of the uncircumcised but one that "confers equality of status" across difference.[14]

She sharpens her feminist focus in her conclusions, asserting a major issue in the Galatians conflict may have been the discomfort of the pro-circumcision group over whether an uncircumcised Jew was, in effect, a "real man." She credits Paul in Galatians 5 and 6 with further disrupting the status quo, citing Paul's challenge to traditional norms for hierarchy in households in relation to the then-expected roles of women and servants.

In the end, however, Kahl concludes Paul's radical notions were too intimidating for Galatian men then, and still, perhaps, for some men today. Thus, she notes, the role and task of servanthood has continued to fall too much on women.

As I reflect on Kahl's commentary on Galatians, I am grateful for the broader perspective it invites, and, at the same time, a deepened capacity to read Scripture through the eyes of contemporary women (as best I can). The feminist view must continue to be lifted up to provoke, challenge, disrupt, and speak in new ways to more traditional Protestants. As with critical race theory in biblical interpretation, this feminist lens has served women—and open-minded men—well, sometimes even to the point of transformation.

Yet, as with Braxton, we may also ask Kahl whether an

even broader, intersectional application of her thinking is in order. While Paul mentions multiple sets of identity in 3:27–28, Kahl offers not even a nod to how gender issues intersect with other aspects of identity. As with Braxton's focus on race, Kahl may be best understood as bringing an urgent feminist voice.

But I wondered what a Caldwell member named Riley would say about Kahl's decision to leave out a more intersectional view. In August 2019, the interfaith worship service that kicks off the annual Pride Week in Charlotte returned to Caldwell church, where it had begun a decade earlier. To a packed sanctuary, Riley, a Charlotte Pride board member, offered the welcome.

She began by saying, "My name is Riley. I am a mixed-race, non-binary, lesbian Christian." The gathered worshipping community applauded. In describing herself, not only did Riley include the fullness of how she sees herself, she gave us a true example of what both/and thinking looks like. (What she could have added is that she is a wife and grandmother raising her mixed-race grandchild, a choir member, an active disciple who rarely misses a Sunday, a child of God, and a sinner redeemed by Christ.)

And what of other both/and people? How may Kahl have spoken to Kevin Martin, who worked with Jesus to broker the resurrection of Caldwell? He's male, African American, and differently abled with multiple sclerosis. Or his white wife, Tovi? Or, perhaps one day when she is older, their adopted biracial daughter?

What about those Caldwell members who are gay men in interracial relationships? Or the transgender woman, a hairdresser who attended church one Sunday in beautifully blended hair of purple and pink?

What would these members, who so sincerely seek to

follow Christ and to recognize themselves in the church, say about single-axis thinking? An intersectional church, or one that tries to see its world more through that lens, may ask questions like this in the future. Could there be a commentary that offers a more dynamic, intersectional reading?

We should not leave feminist reading of Scripture without a brief word about womanist theology. Womanist theology moves closer to intersectional analysis in how it lifts up what Raquel St. Clair calls the "'tridimensional reality' of racism, sexism, and classism."[15] The womanist perspective, St. Clair writes, pursues wholeness, particularly for African American women:

> The struggle of womanist theologians against oppression has to go beyond survival to the liberation and well-being of women. Gender, race, and class intersect and reinforce each other in the lives of African American women. Therefore, womanist theology does not limit itself to sexism and "an analysis of white racism," but also includes issues of class.[16]

Womanist theology thus delves more deeply into a true intersectional analysis, even by St. Clair's definition, taking in the perspective of women who love other women, sexually and platonically.[17]

AN LGBTQ PERSPECTIVE

For an LGBTQ perspective, we turn to two works by Father Patrick Cheng, an author and adjunct faculty at Episcopal Divinity School at Union Theological Seminary. He is now an Episcopal priest, attorney, and affiliated associate professor of theology at Chicago Theological Seminary.

Cheng applies "queer theology," which he defines in these ways: First, as "LGBT people 'talking about God'"; and, second, "theology that talks 'about God' in a self-consciously transgressive manner, especially in terms of challenging societal norms about sexuality." Third, according to Cheng, queer theology erases boundaries and "challenges and deconstructs the natural binary categories of sexual and gender identity."[18]

Underlying all of this is Cheng's foundational idea of "radical love," which he defines as "a love that is so extreme it dissolves existing boundaries."[19] Some of these boundaries are between divine and human, powerful and weak, knowing and unknowing, and sexual and nonsexual relationships.

In Jesus Christ, Cheng writes, we see "the recovery of radical love" after it is rejected in sin and disobedience. Thus, Christ is the embodiment of radical love and atonement is the ending of scapegoating through Christ's activity in radical love.[20] The person of the Holy Spirit is the return to radical love "from which we all came."[21]

Turning to Galatians, Cheng finds insights that can help us hear viewpoints that are subsets of the LGBTQ experience. In his Galatians commentary, Cheng writes, "Galatians can be read as a critique of the dominant white queer culture to the extent that it imposes its own implicit code of conduct or 'law' upon those of us who are also from minority ethnic or cultural backgrounds."

Galatians can be read, he says, to teach us *all* people are loved by God out of the depth of God's grace in Christ. As with the African American and feminist theologians considered earlier, Cheng sees Paul in Galatians as siding with the marginalized. In Paul's confrontation with Peter over whether Peter flip-flopped on his position on circumcision,

Cheng sees a call to "boldly confront the hypocrisy of so-called Christians who exclude LGBTQ people from full membership in the Church."[22]

As for the keystone verses of Galatians 3:27–28, Cheng finds a promise of radical equality that fully invites gay, lesbian, bisexual, queer, and transgender believers into communion with God and the church. Turning to the freedom of the spirit that Paul lifts up in chapter 5 in Galatians, Cheng takes care to add "Paul warns us that this freedom should not be seen as an opportunity for self-indulgence (Galatians 5:13)."[23] Rather, Paul's emphasis is all believers are to become servants to one another and love their neighbor as self. Cheng concludes his commentary with a return to one of his opening points, that Galatians can be seen among LGBTQ people of all ethnic backgrounds as a critique of the dominant white culture within the more broadly diverse LGBTQ community.[24]

As a personal reflection on Cheng, twelve years of ministry with LGBTQ members confirms for me the need to hear perspectives such as Cheng's outside so-called purely "gay churches." The wounds and rejection LGBTQ people carry from negative experiences with the church at large run deep, requiring years of nurture and care in Christ. Theologies such as Cheng's serve a pivotal role in helping LGBTQ people see themselves as wholly standing in God's grace, just as with African American and feminist Christians who have been denigrated by white dominant Christianity. Cheng brings clarity that speaks to the journey of LGBTQ believers who seek the embrace of the church.

For many who haven't read interpretations like Cheng's, this may open our eyes to the complexities of diversity. His focus on the contrast and tension between white gay culture and other gay cultures underscores how far the church must go to understand the dynamics of intersectional analysis and how it can inform the church's role in offering invitation, access, and equality to all.

As with other authors considered in this chapter, however, I also read Cheng to fall short of what could be a fully intersectional perspective. He critiques white LGBTQ folk for othering LGBTQ people of color. To his credit, he does draw a broader circle of inclusion and reads Galatians to embrace all boundaries. But he doesn't explicitly extend his reading of Galatians as more intersectional to include other marginalized groups as seen, for example, through lenses of gender or class.

AN AFRICAN AMERICAN LGBTQ PERSPECTIVE

In his 2006 book *Their Own Receive Them Not*, which was republished in 2010, Episcopal priest Rev. Horace Griffin explores the church's inconsistent views—from historic to current—of racial oppression and the oppression of LGBTQ people, particularly of color. Griffin is now associate pastor at Atlanta's St. Luke's Episcopal and formerly served as associate professor of field education and leadership development at Pacific School of Religion.

Griffin highlights what he calls the hostility of the African American church at large toward homosexuality. He says Black faith leaders apply a "hermeneutic of suspicion" to traditional Eurocentric white interpretations of Scripture on issues of race. Yet, these same leaders, he charges, don't aim that same skepticism at issues of homosexuality. In other words, Black faith leaders have questioned white interpretations of how Scripture addresses race, but they have not applied similar analysis of how the traditional Black church has viewed LGBTQ people.

Griffin stipulates Black preachers and religious leaders have emphasized what they call the "sin" of homosexuality in disproportionate ways. For example, he asserts, too many Black preachers advance what he terms a "heterosexual supremacist" approach to marriage. About same-sex marriage, he writes:

> When there are so many problems in black families and communities—heterosexual male violence in homes, heterosexual fathers absent from the majority of black homes, unfaithful marriages, gang violence . . . it is difficult to understand why black pastors spend so much time opposing gays for honoring their committed relationships by choosing marriage.[25]

Griffin takes issue with another argument he sometimes hears in Black churches, that homosexuality historically was never "native" in Africa. Instead, the argument goes, it was brought to Africa by white colonists. "The cultural teaching that homosexuality is a white perversion provides the convenience of disowning reality in black people."[26] No surprise then that, for decades, Black LGBTQ believers in churches have remained in the closet, unable to be who they are. Two notable such closeted Black LGBTQ persons were Barbara Jordan and James Cleveland, he writes.

More broadly, Griffin offers four categories of those who are LGBTQ in the church:

- *Guilty Passing*: Gays who feel that they deserve the condemnation imposed by the church.
- *Angry Passing*: Those who publicly deny or remain silent but participated in the oppression of gay members.

- *Silent Passing*: Those who deny or remain silent about their reality and pass as heterosexual.
- *Opportunistic Passing*: Those who remain closeted and may or may not participate in the heterosexual supremacy in the Black church.[27]

Turning to the few exceptions when churches have openly welcomed African American LGBTQ people, Griffin highlights the work in the 1990s of the Metropolitan Community Church (MCC) and Unity Fellowship Church as not just fully and openly welcoming but designed to be inclusive sanctuaries for LGBTQ African Americans who feel rejected by the mainstream Black church.[28] These churches provide the particular richness of African American worship without the homophobia—latent or otherwise—of the broader Black faith tradition, including Black Baptist and Pentecostal aspects of worship:

> The development of black gay churches makes it possible for black gay Christians for the first time to hear the gospel in their own ways and reinterpret the gospel in their own context—taking into account both race and sexual orientation at every step in the process.[29]

In turn, these movements can serve as a bridge toward the day when LGBTQ worshippers, both white and people of color, could comprise the same congregation. So it is in the Church of the Open Door in Chicago, Griffin writes. Even there, however, he points out that worship styles and differences in class complicate the shared experience. Another complicating factor is the church's location in an upper-middle-class neighborhood, which feels less comfortable for those in poorer economic circumstances.[30]

Even at the mostly Black Church of the Open Door, he

noted in his 2006 publication, there was no evidence of intentional outreach to white, LGBTQ prospective members, emphasizing the complexity of what an even more diverse church experience requires. The emergence of Black, LGBTQ churches should not, Griffin emphasizes, "prevent lesbians, gays, and heterosexuals from confronting the ongoing black church homophobia and heterosupremacy."[31]

Griffin concludes with a note of hope and a call for a new pastoral attention to the LGBTQ community by the majority, heterosexual Black church: "Some African American pastors are reassessing their stance against lesbian and gay Christians," specifically showing a new readiness to factor in the historical context of the Bible's same-gender references. He calls for Black church leaders to "bring the spirit and flesh together in healthy ways rather than seeing them in dualistic ways and in a never-ending tension."[32]

> My challenge to African Americans is to critically engage the relationship between Christianity and homosexuality in the same faithful way that a critical engagement of Christianity and race is offered. In the inheritance of the black church as the center of black people's lives, black pastors as heirs and keepers of this sacred canopy can lead others in dismantling its sin of homophobia and heterosupremacy.[33]

While Griffin's analysis did not address Galatians or Galatians 3:27–28, it serves to help in many ways. He gives us a window into the journey of LGBTQ African Americans and the specific pain of their twofold rejection—by the society at large and by the traditional Black church.

Given Griffin published this work in 2006, it is important to point out some historic African American denominations have since taken a more inclusive stance. But the fundamental divide remains in many places, including Charlotte.

For years, many LGBTQ people of faith found safety in congregations and denominations, such as the MCC and Unity Fellowship traditions, specifically shaped to welcome them. In more recent years, as the nation itself has become more accepting, some have moved to more diverse congregations, expressing a desire to worship and be in faith-based relationships with more of a cross section of their communities. Caldwell has seen that a good deal and is richly blessed by those who come to worship with a cross section of all of God's children in a safe environment that centers their faith and leadership.

As Griffin points out, however, building more both/and congregations has its tricky parts. Griffin enters a long-running dispute over whether the struggle for equality for LGBTQ people can be called, in whatever way, like that of African Americans. Many passionately deny the two are the same.

In the pulpit and in the press, I have been called out for unknowingly drawing the same parallel even in the broadest outline. I respect the point and submit that, at the end of the day, people of color are best to determine its legitimacy. Critics often point out that race is a purely social construct invented for the oppression of a particular people, gay and otherwise. Sexuality, on the other hand, is proven to be at least in part genetic. Both points are true, but my hope would be one day there can be more of a dialogue between the two populations to build deeper mutual understanding and empathy, one that doesn't have to insist on apples-to-apples comparisons but still can form bonds of partnership against shared power structures.

I need to note that hope is far easier for me to express, given I am from neither population. I acknowledge I have no experience in understanding their shared and respective journeys of being "othered" as they have. But wouldn't that kind of cross-experience dialogue in church be truly intersectional and, thus, enormously beneficial to those of us in the majority to hear as we seek to overcome our various blind spots?

Griffin also helpfully highlights the complexity of the work of groups from marginalized populations. When a congregation gets into this work, it finds there is "diversity within diversity." Black or gay, feminist or trans, an intersectional idea of church takes us out of our silos, but it also corrals many unhealed wounds.

Congregations are called to be spiritual hospitals for injured souls, as I explore in the next chapter. With that, however, comes potentially volatile dynamics and ready triggers for people who have long been overlooked or worse. In the whole, though, encountering a perspective like Griffin's adds to the richness of how we read and interpret Scripture, alongside that of the other "othered" voices we have heard in this chapter.

MORE FULLY EQUIPPED?

"As many of you as were baptized into Christ have clothed yourselves with Christ. There is no longer Jew or Greek, there is no longer slave or free, there is no longer male and female; for all of you are one in Christ Jesus."[34]

Just what *did* Paul mean here? Just what do these verses have to say to the living of our days in this pluralistic age, the dawn of America as a majority-minority nation? Each year on Trinity Sunday, we celebrate the arrival of the Holy

Spirit and depth and breadth of God as seen in the Holy Trinity, Creator, Redeemer, and Sustainer. Through the Trinity, as I like to say at Caldwell, we are "fully equipped" to love and worship God with our full lives.

Perhaps for many disciples, this chapter's encounter with these long-othered voices is jarring. Some may say, "Well, I just can't get there." Perhaps, on the other hand, this brief glimpse of differing interpretations of one passage of Scripture entices them to leave the familiar highways and byways of white, straight, cisgender, male-dominant biblical interpretation and explore other avenues to God's word, love, and justice.

However, this review also shows the remaining tendency, even among scholars, to stay in what may be called their "affinity lane." In each of these examples, these authors hold focus to one segment of the population. As I have pointed out with each, none opens their own interpretation to other marginalized groups. Perhaps the intersectional church of the future can, at least, read them alongside each other to comprise a truly inclusive, intersectional view of what God was up to in Galatia and just how far Paul's words could take us today.

Is the both/and intersectional church a way forward? And just what happens, warts and all, when congregations take up the tricky and liberating work of acting on that notion? These more practical questions are explored in specific in the next chapter through the witness of some intersectional congregations with experience in this work.

6

THE CHURCH
OF BOTH/AND:
JUSTICE AND …
(EVERYTHING)

The apostle Paul calls the church, the body of Christ in the world, to strive to be "all things to all people," a never-ending journey of aspiration. As congregations respond, many tend to become known for some things and not others, either because they choose to emphasize an aspect of ministry or because they are doing something particularly well.

Some churches focus on evangelism, putting energy into sharing the good news of the gospel of Jesus Christ to fill their pews. Some invest deeply in Christian education (or formation). They program a range of well-honed offerings for learners of all ages. Their call is to teach disciples to love the Word and grow in their personal spirituality. A few even have theologians in residence or regularly bring in nationally known speakers and authors.

Other churches focus internally on their members' care and fellowship. Some emphasize building relationships through small groups. Some excel at comforting the bereaved and use telephone trees and online sign-up websites to arrange meals for the sick and recovering. Some invest resources such as pastoral time and attention on aging members, a segment that makes up an ever-growing portion of today's mainline Protestant congregations.

Many churches excel at worship, the one hour or so that the largest part of the congregation is together in person or, as during the COVID-19 pandemic, online or both. Theologically, worship feeds the rest of church life. Worship serves and praises God as it points to Christ to inform, inspire, shape, nurture, and send disciples back into the world. A few mainline Protestant churches reach their communities through commercial television worship, though demand for airtime and pressure on ad revenues are eating away at that soon-to-be old-fashioned idea. The COVID-19 pandemic prodded thousands more congregations to put their worship online. Then there are the multisite and other megachurches that have poured millions of dollars into high-production worship featuring charismatic preachers and rock and roll praise bands.

For most churches, life together isn't complete without mission and service. Some prioritize financial support for local, national, and international causes to serve those in need. Some match their money with the time and talent of people seeking to make a difference as Christ's hands and feet. The outcome may be charity for those in need or reverse evangelism that helps members put their lives in context of the gospel and the world's needs. Less frequently, some portion of the staff time and capacity, church budget, and member energy focuses on long-term, systemic change in the world to bring about the justice that lives at the heart of God's expressed desire for creation.

In their response to God's gift of grace in Christ Jesus, intersectional churches bend their whole being toward justice. For them, as the body of Christ, God's call to justice is the center post on which all else hangs. This is not to say these churches subordinate worship or totally sideline other vital parts of life together in Christ. Their worship is innovative and alive, whether it is traditional or something else. Rather, their entire lives follow the Reformed pattern of Christian living. Everything they do is in response to God's grace in Jesus Christ—but nothing is done without an orientation to justice. The dream of justice is the lifeblood of Christ that animates these churches.

WHY JUSTICE?

Why devote attention to what may seem to some to be only one aspect of life with God? Why risk limiting programmatic offerings and therefore potential new members whose interests may vary more widely? Why not go with a buffet of programming and attract as many newcomers as possible with offerings on spirituality, Bible study, what makes for a successful marriage, how to raise children, and on and on? All valid questions.

For some, teaching, preaching, and working for justice is to "get political," the deadly "third rail" of church life. It's true that a church can focus on justice for only so long and only so often before upsetting someone. Members and visitors may have a different political view than the one they infer from the preaching or the teaching. It's also true that justice work sounds to some like it is too messy, too exhausting, or too intangible and unsatisfying in today's short-attention-span consumer culture.

Why justice, then? Because justice lives at the center of God's heart. Because in more than two thousand biblical references to justice, God calls us to make it the bedrock of any community. Communities of any size, whether a couple or a family, a nation or a world, are diseased without inherent fairness and balance. A Christ-centered faith is hollow without recognizing inclusivity and justice lived at the heart of Jesus's ministry.

From Genesis to Revelation, Scripture attests to God's vision for a just community. The Ten Commandments outline what God wants for us in life together centered on God. The prophets decry the Israelites' false sense of what worship looks like.[1]

In Christ, we see God's self-revelation, a desire to reach all kinds of people but with an unmistakable preference for the poor, the sick, the wounded, and the outsiders. The Beatitudes in the Sermon on the Mount paint a vivid picture certainly not of the world as it is today, not of the kingdom of God in heaven alone, but of the kingdom on earth according to God's dream for us. Paul's letters and other epistles speak to community in Christ. The Godhead creates the world for peace and wholeness, but humanity has other ideas. God came in Christ to teach and preach, challenging the Roman Empire's ways of oppression and suppression as well as the stultifying legalism of the Pharisees. Christ died in our stead and was resurrected to be our hope. The Holy Spirit comes, making the difference between the chaos of Babel and the wonder of Pentecost.

What does the world show us in response? Gaps between what God wants and how things are. The race gap. The wealth gap. The gender gap. The gap between the hopeful and the hopeless. The gap between nations amid wars and conflict. The gap between political ideologies, deepening every day. The gap between the assurance of God and so many fears of the future that fuel movements like religious extremism and white supremacy.

One can add to the list what one sees around them. The sum is the gap between the already and the not yet, Christ's entrance into the world and the more perfect fulfillment of God's vision. These gaps measure the injustice that Christ exposed in his life and teachings, his death and resurrection.

Some don't feel compelled to act; it's too much to stand in that gap or their personal piety is sufficient unto itself. They wait on Christ's return and tell themselves the inherent brokenness of the world is too far gone to fix. Many say God alone can fix the world's brokenness and faith is supposed to be about personal salvation. Others pray . . . and pray and pray.

Most Christians, it seems, would just as soon avoid getting too chummy in all of this. They prefer transactional responses over relational ones. A 2019 Barna Group study asked, "In what ways are you most frequently generous to others?" Only 25 percent responded with "emotional/relational support" while the remainder favored "gifts," "monetary support," "volunteering/service," "hospitality," or "other."[2] We wonder why America is so divided and distant from itself, its own people. Perhaps our avoidance of authenticity and vulnerability in relationships is a clue. Without more empathy, how can we close the gaps that divide us?

The churches I highlight that aspire to intersectional Christianity feel called to stand in the world's gaps with *all* they are. The pursuit of justice—also called "righteousness" in Scripture—centers their care, fellowship, faith formation, outreach, evangelism, and worship. At these churches, active participation in bringing God's justice to the world is not just a department or a committee of a dedicated few. It is the heartbeat of the whole church. This chapter lifts up the voices of these churches' pastors.

JUSTICE AND THEOLOGY

How do these intersectional churches describe their theology?

- "Traditional, with a splash of progressive, plus some African American perspective."
- "Takes Scripture seriously, social justice passionately, valuing progressive/prophetic words and actions and prioritizing visible actions/ministries that reflect biblical justice."
- "Radical! And relational."
- "A 'focus statement' of 'Love God, love neighbor.' All the rest is detail."
- "Seeking to find a better future faithful to the great witness of the past but realizing that no past holds the reign of God in its fullness."
- "Thoroughly Presbyterian—i.e., the will of God is best discerned through the community's experience with God."

These churches work to balance perspectives, even as they take on issues some deem controversial, and read the gospel in what some would call progressive ways.

At First Presbyterian of Brooklyn, New York, Rev. Adriene Thorne describes its theology as "progressive, inclusive, and wrestling with making space for those outside that circle, as they are conservative members." At this church, "theology is informed by liberation theology—womanist theology in particular."

But these approaches to theology can create tension. Several of the churches I studied, and my own, feel an obligation to make a safe space for people with politically or theologically conservative perspectives, but they say that can be tricky. The sign out front at Caldwell says, "God invites. We welcome. All." But we have been seen as falling short on that promise when theologically or politically conservative-leaning visitors don't feel so welcomed. We preach justice, not partisan politics, but our preaching can sound like that to some. We do not endorse political candidates, but we do hold elected officials accountable to lead morally and for all Americans, not just the few.

Caldwell does have centrist and conservative members and I salute them for their desire to be in a community where their views may not always be represented each Sunday. Charlotte is full of fine and well-led "purple" churches where they may feel more comfortable, but these hearty souls come to Caldwell for something different.

At the end of the day, however, intersectional churches feel called to be something new and needed. "If diversity is to be valued, then the dominant cultural narrative has to be challenged and questioned through the sharing of others' experiences," said Rev. Dr. Randy Bush, pastor at East Liberty Presbyterian in Pittsburgh.

JUSTICE AND CONGREGATIONAL CARE

Justice-rooted care is both/and.

It is casseroles on the doorstep and cards in the mail when adversity visits members. It is sitting with the dying and grieving with the grieving. It is rejoicing with couples as they plan to be married or have children. It is sitting with couples when they struggle and, when necessary, helping to bring a just and faithful end to relationships that fail. It is celebrating lives when they end and, for the living, remembering Christ defeated death for all time.

And . . . it is walking with members who limp through life at times, visibly or not. For those who have enough, it is coming to understand what it means to not have enough. It is about empathy that transcends one's own experience to understand the wounds and scars of those who carry them, whether those wounds came at the hands of family, society, church, or something else.

In his book *In Living Color: An Intercultural Approach to Pastoral Care and Counseling*, Emanuel Lartey offers multiple models of pastoral care that apply especially to what he calls cross-cultural congregations:

- Pastoral care as therapy, that heals or makes members feel better; pastoral care as acts of ministry, proclamation, teaching, prophecy, service, fellowship, administration, and worship;
- Pastoral care as social action, prophecy that speaks truth to power; pastoral care as empowerment, recognizing what is good and of worth and value within each member and assisting in the "conscientization" of members who are oppressed and marginalized; and,
- Pastoral care as interaction, using "relational skills" to "assist people, explore, clarify, and change unwanted thoughts, feelings, and behavior."[3]

In diverse, inclusive congregations, care for members and friends must aspire to be all the above. In the cohort studied for this book, the mostly white congregations that aspire to be intersectional, this work requires an inversion of the "usual" church idea of pastoral care. It is not "fast food," however much pressure church staffs and budgets may be under to try to provide care by scale. It is highly specific and personalized. It is what Lartey calls "interculturality," whose maxim is "Every human person is in some respects (a) like all others (b) like some others (c) like no other."[4]

Care in these congregations is both individualized and with the whole in mind. Intersectional congregations seek to gather and converge people in populations who have been the targets of prejudice, hate, abuse, racism, homophobia, transphobia, classism, and the cancerous effects of generational poverty. That means congregational care, as with all intersectional ministry, is anything but clean and clinical. Rather, it is gloriously messy. When a church seeks to be a hospital for weary and wounded souls, as St. Augustine commended, the hurt can spill out in multiple directions.

It also means the lane dividers between types of ministry in the church go away. Everything bears witness to God's vision for equality and wholeness. Intersectional congregations are in the hope business because hope heals. In *Injustice and the Care of Souls*, Sheryl A. Kujawa-Holbrook and Karen B. Montagno write: "Antiracist pastoral care is based in hope."[5] They name the "interlocking nature of oppression" and its truth that "it is not possible to address fully one form of oppression and not another."[6]

So, for the church of both/and, justice work is more than just anti-racist, as urgent, heavy, and ongoing as that work is. It is anti-poverty, anti-homophobia and anti-myopia of the heart of any kind that subtracts from achieving God's vision of justice for *all* God's children. Care comes in the form of staff and leaders knowing this and being prepared to be an agent of hope and healing to members in all sorts of personal crises.

Sometimes, justice-based care leads to unexpected relationships and liberating forms of healing for all involved. When Lucy was released from prison after sixteen years, she settled at Rutba House, an intentional community in Durham rooted in justice and neighbor. Someone there thought she may find community at Durham Presbyterian Church. The congregation embraced her as she got her life on track. Still, one thing remained, her longing for her life partner, who was still behind bars. To close that gap, Rev. Franklin Golden performed the first same-gender wedding between women in a North Carolina prison. The church met her in her specific need. Lucy tells Rev. Golden she trusts three groups of people—her housemates at Rutba House, those she came to know in prison, and Durham Presbyterian Church.

Now, Lucy is reaching back to help another, leading the church's advocacy for a man in prison whom the church has come to know. The advocacy efforts helped shorten his sentence, giving him hope and a supportive community that prays for him. Relational care across differences leads to new mission.

"The care is determined by each relationship," Golden reflected. "We don't talk about things so much as we love and try to stay close to whoever shows up."

Justice-oriented care, hope, and healing happens when those who are wounded and hope-starved see their church marching in the Pride parade *and* in the Martin Luther King Jr. holiday parade as a sign of one long-oppressed group helping to bear the burdens and speak up for another. It comes when marginalized members see others withstanding racist and homophobic picketers who try to block people from coming into worship. It happens when preaching names injustice, when members march in the streets to protest a bad police shooting, and when a church raises money for the support of families affected by HIV/AIDS.

Care, hope, and healing rooted in justice come about when poorer congregation members, those a paycheck or less away from the streets, see their church open a homeless shelter and embrace its residents fully in the life of the church. Healing occurs when those who have known generations of oppression and rejection see their church teach children to build a better future of open-minded inclusion and provision.

Hope and healing happen when members without cars are not left out of activities or meetings, when communications don't assume everyone has online access, when the choir director understands not all choir members read well and adapts accordingly. Hope and healing occur when all kinds of voices, but particularly those not usually invited into the center, are elevated to leadership. As with casseroles for the sick, homemade finger sandwiches, and iced tea at receptions for funerals; as with pastors making house calls "just because," the church of both/and cares for the marginalized by giving them hope in all the ways its members bear witness across the traditional "lanes" of ministry and care.

JUSTICE AND CHRISTIAN FORMATION

In the middle of the last century, perhaps the most vivid snapshot of the vibrancy of life in Protestant churches was the buzz in the Sunday school building. Virtually every church had one—a wing, a basement hallway under the sanctuary, or a freestanding building. At Caldwell, when the congregation was at its height of twelve hundred members, it extended the original education building twice to catch up with the growing flock and its hunger for how Sunday school—in those days—blended community and teaching.

In 1949, Caldwell elder W. E. Price was elected moderator of the General Assembly of the Presbyterian Church in the United States (the PCUS, or Southern Presbyterian denomination). With denomination-wide responsibilities for church polity and mission, this was a vaunted role for any leader. But Price considered his title of Sunday school superintendent at Caldwell to be even more important, gathering attendance reports for each class and awarding silver dollar coins to youth communicants who could recite The Shorter Catechism. In his era, adults taught, children shined their shoes, and everyone carried their Bibles. The Stronghold Class at Caldwell was even broadcast on WBT Radio, the region's most powerful station, extensive in its range and reach.

All that was what Christian education looked like last century, when Christianity rested comfortably in the American mainstream culture. In contrast, amid a very different, secular culture, today's resurrected Caldwell has sustained one traditional Sunday school class over the last decade. That reflects national trends, where fewer than one in ten active members attend a traditional Sunday school class, as defined by the hour or so before 11:00 a.m. worship. So, as in many churches, Caldwell supplements with a range of other short and intermediate offerings to help people deepen their knowledge of God in Christ, in faith, and in public witness. Because the Sunday-school hour is no longer a fixture for families, we design these offerings to have a specific focus and meet at times and in places members can fit into their busy lives.

At Caldwell, Christian formation still happens in all sorts of ways. The Faith Walkers, formerly the "Women's Circle" but now coed, gathers on Wednesday mornings. Another group deeply invested in racial reconciliation meets on Mondays to read and discuss books on that topic and what their faith demands. The church hosts citywide public forums on public issues that intersect with faith, theology, and mission; and Scripture, current affairs, and recent books are discussed and debated at breweries and coffee-houses nearer the homes of our members. Recently, everything has gone online due to COVID-19 and many of those new skills and ways of gathering are part of our expanded offerings. But the days when more people attended Sunday school than worship in the American church are never coming back.

So, spaces built for traditional classroom education are being used to educate and form Christians in other ways. Over these twelve years in resurrection, the Caldwell congregation has repeatedly asked, "How can we best use our twelve-thousand-square-foot W. E. Price Education Building to serve God and our city?"

God has answered, positioning us to use it as a bilingual preschool, a homeless shelter, and a "24-7" urban prayer space, open night and day to the general public. Next, we will renovate it to become affordable apartments for several disadvantaged populations in response to Charlotte's affordable housing crisis.

The W. E. Price Education Building has served as an incubator for ministries in their start-up and "toddler" phases, the church's and its partners'. Far from sitting around tables to hear a lesson, each of these opportunities has created hands-on learning and living curriculum. Each provides incarnational spaces that educate members of all ages and stages in how the justice gap in our city can be addressed.

Even though Caldwell and thousands of other churches have repurposed their classrooms, we haven't mothballed our minds and fired all the teachers in our midst. God still calls us to use our minds, as good Presbyterians always have, with justice at the center. We've gathered to watch the acclaimed PBS *Eyes on the Prize* civil rights documentary as a model for action. We invited seminary and college profes-sors to lead a six-week class on "Seeing Our Whiteness." We hosted a six-week series led and taught by transgender people for those seeking to support them.

We've studied how well-intended church work can become charity that fails to address root issues, and thus risks perpetuating systemic and structural inequalities and inequities. We read and discuss books that challenge the status quo and remind us that Jesus did the same. We part-ner with Union Presbyterian Seminary's Center for Social Justice and Racial Reconciliation to offer speakers and pub-lic forums. None of this is unique or groundbreaking, but it is what putting justice at the core of Christian formation looks like for us.

A particular calling for Caldwell has been to become a teaching campus. In twelve years, Caldwell has welcomed and supervised more than thirty interns in ministry, most from the Charlotte campus of Union Presbyterian Semi-nary but also from area colleges and other seminaries. We launched the Gambrell Hope Internships in Social Justice, an eight-week immersive summer experience for five college students a year to work at area justice-oriented organiza-tions and to walk with Caldwell as we seek to learn and act. The education goes both ways as these students share their journeys with us and open our eyes and hearts to all they learn about what justice looks like in our city.

What about other churches aspiring to practice justice-centered, intersectional forms of faith and service?

At Brown Memorial Park Avenue Presbyterian (Baltimore), mission and learning are inseparable in how it invests both in community organizing. It is a founding member of Baltimoreans United in Leadership Development (BUILD), a broad-based, nonpartisan, interfaith, multiracial power organization in Baltimore City. BUILD is a network of congregations and other organizations that listens to its membership, develops local leaders, and seeks social change with and alongside its people. It focuses on systemic issues, including living wages, affordable housing, and improvements to Baltimore City Schools. In these and other ways, Brown Memorial educates its members about God's vision for justice by bearing public witness.

Brown Memorial's Rev. Andrew Foster Connors explains its education in mission is "primarily through our community organizing, but also through public actions on marriage equality, peacemaking and war resistance, and interfaith dialogue and work. Our worship grounds that work, understanding each member of the church as a 'missionary' sent into the world in our daily lives to pursue God's justice in our daily activities and vocations."

Down the interstate in Washington, DC, Church of the Pilgrims has another take on justice-centered Christian formation. It uses its large, original education wing as home to The Pilgrimage, a hostel and seminar center hosting groups from around the country—all ages, faith-based and not, from across the Christian tradition. The Pilgrimage has become a rite of passage for many churches' youth groups and confirmation classes, and inspired similar programs at other churches.

"We believe young people can be agents of change in their communities," says its director Rachel Pacheco. "The Pilgrimage facilitates service-learning experiences around poverty, homelessness, hunger, and advocacy. People make a pilgrimage to DC, the nation's capital, to see beyond the museums and monuments and federal government to understand the reality of people living on the street in the shadow of the Capitol building."[7]

Groups volunteer, listen to stories, sit and talk with people, and learn about where God is serving the vulnerable amid the District of Columbia's displacement of the marginalized. Through these experiences, groups break down stereotypes, work with people who are different, and learn how to engage the advocacy process.

"It's an opportunity to follow the way of Jesus by seeing people we usually ignore or avoid and recognizing the face of Jesus in our neighbors experiencing homelessness," Pacheco says. "It's about building beloved community by reaching across the barriers that society builds to divide us and opening ourselves to a new understanding of the world through listening to someone else's experience. We need to relearn how to love our neighbors as Jesus showed us."

JUSTICE AND WORSHIP

Intersectional churches take worship seriously, including its opportunity to show worshippers what justice and shared, equitable leadership look like. That doesn't mean strident, righteously indignant sermons week after week. It also certainly doesn't mean aligning theology or Christian identity to any party ideology, or subordinating ministry and mission to the American flag.

In worship, justice looks like a diverse array of ordained and unordained people, today's urban America and tomorrow's America, leading worship. It means ensuring a diverse set of voices read and interpret the Scripture, not just a special guest preacher one or two times a year. It means that I, as white, cisgender head of staff, yield the pulpit to women and people of color almost as often as I can.

Justice-centered worship also has a sound and a blended rhythm. It sounds like a range of music, traditional but also Black gospel, African American spirituals, and global music that makes congregants think and feel as they sing. Contemporary or praise music doesn't seem to fit. Most intersectional churches go with a range between traditional and blended worship music.

"Our choir can show up and sing a classical piece and then shift to gospel," says Rev. Andrew Foster Connors at Brown Memorial. "Our preachers can preach in 'white style' worship and shine in the Black church call-and-response tradition. In other words, we bring an adaptability that challenges others. I think this helps us in our overall decision-making at a time when the contemporary church is forced to be more flexible overall."

Worship in diverse and intersectional churches opens us to see our gathering to praise God and hear the Word in new and liberating ways. Among Presbyterians and other Reformed traditions, those in the majority are invited to come to know worship from what is likely to be a new perspective. For three decades, Rev. Nibs Stroupe and his wife, Caroline Leach, led a forerunner in this work at Oakhurst Presbyterian, Atlanta, where the congregation was half white and half Black. There they witnessed the power of worship long at the center of the African American tradition, a faith that sustained African Americans through centuries of oppression. They write:

> The Presbyterian God has often been a stern God, a God who almost delights in crushing sinners, a God who will get us unless we do right. Although one of our founders, John Calvin, indicated that our chief purpose is to glorify God and enjoy God forever, Presbyterians are not often accused of enjoying God in worship in a glorious manner. The African American tradition brings a sense of celebration to American religious life, a sense of affirming in body and mind that God is at the center of our lives, that God has claimed us as daughters and sons, that the presence of God can be enjoyed.[8]

In diverse and intersectional congregations, justice-rooted worship calls on everyone to be flexible and open to learning each Sunday. But it also requires understanding the special burden placed on the people of color who choose each week to come to a majority white church community. I've come to appreciate in ever-deepening ways the sacrifice our members of color make to comprise the minority in our pews. On Sundays when most African Americans worship with each other, finding a particular kind of sanctuary away from their days at work in white-led organizations and institutions, members of color in majority-white congregations must make the added effort to come into what may not feel like "their" space, despite how hard we try. Their fortitude and commitment often go unnoticed and underappreciated.

The corollary to this is white folks need to get in the habit of receiving the gift of new worship styles and cultural norms. For worship to be equal opportunity in how it feeds us, everyone needs to be willing to go with the flow. Fully inclusive worship means stretching members' comfort zones on a regular basis.

As with other intersectional churches, worship at Caldwell usually runs seventy-five to ninety minutes. It includes several times of silence, but the first thirty minutes are highly interactive, including time with children. Caldwell passes the peace for seven to eight minutes, roaming all over our sanctuary to say words so many in so many walks of life desperately need to hear, "The peace of Christ be with you."

The resurrected Caldwell congregation has always applauded in worship, something I hadn't experienced at the traditional churches where I had belonged as a member. But I hear this response as genuine praise and gratitude to God for what worshippers have just heard or experienced rather than a response to a performance. My sense when I visit other churches or worship in large groups, such as conferences, is more and more people are applauding in worship now where once it was forbidden.

Caldwell's music builds on Smitty Flynn's three decades–long experience in leading (as a volunteer!) one of the city's best gospel choirs, first at Seigle Avenue Presbyterian and, since its resurrection, at Caldwell. Caldwell's worship is, in many ways, defined by our choir and music as they authentically lift up spirituals, Black gospel classics, and other movement songs with subversive lyrics that feed our members' sense of call. In the choir, the city's top Google executive sings with a voice that shakes the stained-glass windows. Alongside her are a member who lives in supportive housing, a psychology professor, one of the original Caldwell's few remaining senior saints leaning on her cane, a few attorneys, and a big-hearted chef-laborer-jack-of-all-trades who always seems to make ends meet but, because of his generosity to others, is never in the clear for long.

A few years ago, we hired Anne Hunter Eidson as minister of music, a lifetime progressive Baptist with experience in diverse churches. To inform that search, before her arrival, we held open dialogues with the congregation about what they would like to experience (we always try to start important conversations and decision-making from the bottom up). Keep the gospel, they said, but let's experiment more widely. Today, music at Caldwell is both/and, all the above and more. We sing from the traditional PC(USA) hymnal and a supplemental volume of hymns from the African American tradition. African drums, a baby grand piano, and a refurbished pipe organ carry the tune. On one Sunday, members tap their toes to bluegrass music. On another, Presbyterian-ordained, now retired Zach Thomas gifts us with his best guitar-strumming Woody Guthrie imitation, singing his version of theologically based protest songs when the Empire seems too much to be winning.

Worship is also communal. Rather than relying on members and friends to read all the emails and digital newsletters, we do verbal announcements before worship rather than asking folks to read written announcements in the bulletin. This takes time, and some members periodically complain, but verbal announcements by members from the sanctuary floor convey to all present how members own and lead our ministries and mission. Our roaming passing of the peace came from the old Caldwell remnant and was sewn into our worship style by my predecessor, Rev. Dr. Charlie MacDonald.

About twice a month, we gather joys and concerns from the floor before we offer the prayer for the people. That practice came with the Seigle Avenue diaspora who gave

Caldwell new life and, when needed, we exchange joys and concerns online via Zoom chat to adapt to realities imposed by the COVID-19 pandemic. When it's in person, it takes time too. Still, the chance to hear individual members' prayer concerns connects us through the nitty-gritty truth of all our lives. It gives us a chance to pray for specific members and circumstances by name through the week and reminds us all of our need for God's grace and embrace.

The result of this intentional mishmash is that not everyone loves every aspect of worship. Many would prefer written and online announcements. Some introverts would like it if we just stood in place and passed the peace. Others wish we would drop the moderated joys and concerns, which often features the same voices. We talk about the length of worship at frequent intervals. Each time, the Worship Committee and the Session (board of elders) look for refinements but generally stand pat on worship length, format, and flow. As more couples come with young children, we are mindful that anything past an hour is asking a lot of little ones. But we try to balance these trade-offs to remain welcoming and at least somewhat familiar to all kinds of people, if not a little odd to some at the same time.

I illustrated this commitment a few years ago after finding a 1960s-era hand-cranked mixer in the drawers of one of our kitchens. No doubt, it was used last century to beat eggs for the breakfast gatherings of the Women of the Church or to mix cake batter for parties for the children. In worship, after confessing our sinful tendency to lapse into the "same-old" in the worship and service of God, I put the blades of the mixer into the baptismal font and cranked like a madman to invoke the Holy Spirit to help us keep the waters of our baptism churning in worship.

JUSTICE AND LANGUAGE

Intersectional churches also realize language matters. Doctrine has its place, but not dogma stuffed down worshippers' throats. Openness and exploration mark these churches. For congregations to deepen in their diversity, worshippers of all types and hues need to recognize themselves, their lives, their struggles, and their questions in worship.

For example, I've yet to find definitive proof that God is male. What I do know is many women yearn to connect more deeply with their Creator but, for a variety of reasons, struggle with exclusively male language for the Lord. So I decided to use *only* feminine pronouns to refer to the Divine for the year 2017, the first year of Donald Trump's presidency. That year stretched the congregation and me. I heard from many women who expressed gratitude for the unexpected comfort that came with our year with "her" and "she," which is now a regular mainstay for us, among other expressions for the Lord.

Not long after that, with inclusivity in mind, we stretched again. At the initiative of the committee that leads Caldwell's LGBTQ ministry, we adopted a policy to use nonbinary language. After study by the Worship, Missions and Justice and Discovery and Engagement Committees, the session adopted the following:

1. That Caldwell strive to make the language used in worship more inclusive.
2. That Caldwell use these language changes as teaching points during worship.
3. That Caldwell strive to use more inclusive language in its website and in other online and printed communications.

All of this was to advance our mission to make church safe again for those whom the church had wounded. Lisa Raymaker, the straight, remarkably knowledgeable, focused, and capable elder who led us through this process, explained it this way in a letter to the congregation:

> People who identify as LGBTQ are looking and listening for certain things in order to feel comfortable and fully welcomed in a space. People who identify as trans and nonbinary, especially, listen for language that respects their gender identity and look for people who accept them as they are.
>
> We are working to make the language we use to refer to each other more inclusive. An example could be instead of saying "brothers and sisters in Christ" we may say "beloved" or "family in Christ." Instead of inviting boys and girls to the children's sermon, we may say "young people" or "children." This is one more way for us to practice radical welcome and show God's unconditional love for and acceptance of all people.

As important as anything, we remind ourselves again and again that this is an aspiration. We will get it wrong, a lot, at first—I as much as anyone as I try to rewire my mind and heart around new verbal patterns against those so deeply conditioned by my environment.

"This is a work in progress, and we will learn together as we go," Lisa reminds us. "We all still maintain our own identities, whatever they may be. Now we are just sharing our space with others."

We recognize others will vigorously disagree. "God made Adam and Eve, not Adam and Steve," the counterpoint goes. Other critics will focus on what they perceive as the irrational randomness of gender fluidity. Still others will say this only advances the identity politics they perceive as causing our nation's deep divisions. These practices also expose us to some who take their disagreement to an extreme. We've been regularly picketed on Sundays by fundamentalist, homophobic Christians before. One Sunday morning, we arrived to find the city sidewalk at the foot of our sanctuary steps covered with neat, block lettering conveying messages like, "Love Warns! Tell the truth, Pastor!" (They were not admiring my theology.)

Why "risk" it?

Because, as the PC(USA) General Assembly affirmed in a resolution adopted in 2018, the church has "participated in systemic and targeted discrimination against transgender people, and we have been complicit in violence against them."

Because God's call for justice doesn't leave out any of God's children. And, because lives are at stake. Consider:

- Trans, queer, and nonbinary people can lose up to 90 percent of their relationships with friends and family when they live as their authentic selves.
- Trans people are four times more likely to live in poverty.
- Forty to 50 percent of trans youth will have attempted suicide by the age of twenty, compared to 1.6 percent of the general population.
- Seventy-eight percent of trans youth experience some sort of harassment at school.
- Trans and nonbinary people, especially youth, who have at least one support system (family or school or church or other organization) reduce their risk of suicide to 4 percent.

Would we stand by if we read these data about any other subset of our society? We understand making worship this inclusive is not for everyone. Most churches chose not to conduct same-gender marriages. Other mainline Protestant congregations condemn LGBTQ people outright. Still, others want to welcome God's queer children but they confess their lack of know-how or are still figuring out all that is involved in turning the words on the sign "All are welcome" into reality in the pews. Organizations like the Covenant Network of Presbyterians and More Light Presbyterians stand ready with advice and resources for those who want to begin or advance this journey.

What our congregation has experienced in a decade of expanding God's call with inclusivity and hospitality, as well as advocacy and public witness, is that our towns and cities are full of LGBTQ people who desperately seek a community of faith where they can walk with God alongside others and where they can serve as the hands and feet of Christ without judgment or rejection. Once they feel accepted and healed, these disciples become tireless, deeply committed workers in God's vineyard.

Justice-centered worship is, thus, many things. Each intersectional church has its own version, but common traits are diversity in leadership, a range of music styles, intentional theology in preaching and liturgy, comfort with taking some risks, and leaving plenty of room for the Holy Spirit to blow and dance where it will.

As Rev. Adriene Thorne says: "We allow space for whatever happens to come along on any given Sunday. Rarely do things go as planned, and people don't get bent out of shape about it! It's a beautiful thing."[9]

JUSTICE, DIVERSITY, AND NEW MEMBER OUTREACH

Each intersectional church has its own mix of diversity and its own idea of how—and with whom—to expand its member base. Most of the cohort churches expressed a desire to broaden membership beyond their current diversity. In response to whether their congregations sought particular types of members, answers included:

- The pastor of The Avenue in Charlotte, which is largely LGBTQ and all people of color, wrote: "I'm seeking more white members but don't seek majority white."
- For East Liberty in Pittsburgh: "Unchurched or 'nones' segment of population disenfranchised from typical congregations. Also continued outreach to African American, Latinx, and bicultural groups in our neighborhood as well as a wider range of economic groups."
- Other responses listed "LGBTQ youth," "more transgender families, more children and youth, more Asian and Latinx families."

Four churches I researched said they do not have "targeted" population segments in mind, including these responses:

- The Church of the Pilgrims: "Whoever walks through our doors is who we are."
- At Durham Presbyterian Church, the pastor of its majority-white congregation notes: "We are always at risk of becoming whiter than we desire. . . . We always stay mindful of who is in the room, but we don't have a strategy for making it different. Our thinking is that God gives the

growth—the Spirit draws people together. Diversity is always a sign of that."
- The pastor of Capitol Heights Presbyterian in Denver added: "We need a good 'anyone' who finds us helpful."

JUSTICE AND INTERNAL COMMUNITY BUILDING

With such deep commitment to causes beyond their sanctuary doors, these churches also know the risk of losing their balance. If taken seriously, no church work is easy. Because it is seen by some as controversial and offensive (as with the gospel itself), justice work is particularly edgy, demanding, and exhausting. Those who take it up, individually and collectively, do well to feed and nurture themselves through the ways they build community within the congregation. Community building occurs when congregants spend social time together, but justice work requires more than that. It must be rooted in open, honest, and vulnerable relationship building and relationship deepening that, over time, builds trust.

In these churches, what we once called "fellowship" looks more like telling each other's stories and listening deeply for the truth within each person's story. It looks like getting together to attend performances or watch movies that take on substantive topics related to faith and justice. It looks like multigenerational gatherings rooted in Scripture, where a variety of opinions, perspectives, and approaches are shared aloud and where those who hold power do more listening than talking.

When these foundations are not built and fortified, inter-sectional, missional churches can become frayed and frag-mented amid difficulty, disagreement, or conflict. External pressures, such as living through Trump's America or the tragedy of gun violence and repeated mass shootings, become silent threats whose sheer psychological weight can undermine life together. Before we know it, we've let these worldly yokes drag us down. We start meeting in our sepa-rate factions in the parking lot, where nothing good usually happens.

As missional churches, these congregations are leanly staffed. A related risk for them and any highly engaged mis-sional church comes when a disproportionate share of the church work falls on the same sets of shoulders, tiring the few, running them ragged, and causing them to grow cynical and negative. At Caldwell, the gift of starting over with a clean slate in 2007 allowed us to set several guiding prin-ciples in place that still chart our course. We began with a promise that we would do all we could to engage as many members who were ready and willing in the work of the church. (Some come here to heal and aren't ready; others may not be able or healthy enough in mind, body, or spirit to be asked to take on active responsibility. But anyone can pray!) The goal is to avoid lapsing into the "80/20 norm" of how things get done, where 20 percent of the people (or fewer!) do 80 percent of the work (or more!).

At key intervals over the last twelve years, when Caldwell seems dangerously stretched or at risk of tipping toward the 80/20 norm, we have informally audited the church's capac-ity. We look at each of the 350 or so names in our faith com-munity, determine their current engagement (considering health, readiness, desire, and ability) and test where we are on a range of 0 percent (no one doing anything) and 100 percent (every member actively engaged in two or more ministries).

As with a tachometer gauge on the car dashboard, we test the "motor" to see if it's running too high, which only leads to burnout or worse, or if it's running too low, meaning we have room to increase the capacity of what we do in Christ's name. We adjust the scope of our ministry endeavors to bring things back to a reasonable, sustainable run rate, or we recruit new disciples to engage and fire up the leadership development pipeline. My number-one rule for elders and volunteers is "No burnout!" and I urge them to monitor themselves and come to me to ask for help before they fade away, exhausted.

JUSTICE AND RESOURCES IN MISSION

The churches I studied have wide-ranging initiatives in mission, reflecting the breadth of members' interests and passions. Because of their missional nature, they attract members with above-average levels of energy and activism. In fact, given their diverse membership, passions, and interests in ministry, intersectional churches sometimes encounter tension over which initiatives to emphasize, as well as difficulty with "bandwidth" limitations of both members and staff. These intersectional congregations use their campuses as platforms and enablers of ministry to and for the community. They are active ecumenically and in interfaith partnerships.

As for size and resources, the current average mean membership in the PC(USA) is seventy and the average mean annual budget is $142,868.[10] But these intersectional churches come in all sizes and, interestingly, most are above average in membership size. Among the churches in the cohort I studied, the smallest had an active membership of forty and the largest of 717 at the time of my research in 2017. Their annual budgets ranged from $37,000 to $2.5 million with regular contributions making up by far the largest part of that income. Three congregations drew income from endowments while the other churches supplemented income with building rental and usage fees.

The staffing structures, and thus, in large measure, the capacity of these congregations to support their members and offer outward-focused mission ministries, range according to their size and budgets. Two have more than one pastor, two have part-time clergy, and the remaining congregations have one full-time clergy plus various full-time and part-time staff for music, youth, property management, and business administration. At the time of the study, the Church of the Pilgrims funded 1.5 staff positions through fees from groups coming to stay at The Pilgrimage, its service-experience hostel.

These churches represent different views on how to define what portion of their financial budgets go to what has traditionally been called mission ministry. So, arriving at an apples-to-apples comparison is difficult. That said, while self-sustaining, they exist as much or more for their communities as for their members. These churches strive to be missional, not just mission oriented. Their pursuit of justice transcends the focus of a committee or a subgroup of members. It engulfs their identity and qualifies their use of every dollar and staff resource.

As explored in this chapter, justice is holistic for these congregations. Even then, as I explore in the next chapter, major considerations about how far we must go, and in what order, must be made.

7

THE BOTH/AND
OF REPAIR AND
RECONCILIATION

"Reconciliation! How can you even talk about reconciliation?"

The member of Caldwell Church was deeply upset. She had seen enough, too much actually. Too many police shootings of unarmed, young Black men, too many racist attacks on then-President Barack Obama, and the early signs of how white nationalism would later unapologetically break out into the open under President Donald Trump. As an African American woman who knew trauma firsthand, she wanted to hear no more talk about reconciliation, including in my prayers and sermons.

"Reconciliation!" she said to me one day over coffee. "How can you even talk about reconciliation?"

I was listening but not really hearing what she was saying. Raised in the Reformed tradition, I knew reconciliation as a doctrine and a mainstay of my faith and hope. Long before I'd read Karl Barth's Doctrine of Reconciliation, as if by osmosis, I'd absorbed the good news through sermons and

121

Sunday school that we are reconciled to God through Christ. In Christ, to use language we'd come to love at Caldwell, God stood in the gap of sin for us and refused to let us become estranged. Wasn't this the very heart of Paul's radical, mind-bending claim in Galatians 3:27–28, after all, that because of how Christ reconciled us broken sinners to God once and for all, we are free to pursue the promise of unity amid the glory of our diversity?

We at Caldwell had come to love how our denomination's Confession of 1967 expressed this hope. While written for the social revolution of the 1960s, it speaks so vividly of what we are still experiencing in our national life. As regularly as any creed or confession, we use it as our Affirmation of Faith on Sundays for the promise of its multiple claims that:

> "God's reconciling love breaks down every form of discrimination based on racial or ethnic difference"; "God's reconciliation in Jesus Christ is the ground of the peace, justice, and freedom among nations, which all powers of government are called to serve and defend"; "The church, in its own life, is called to practice the forgiveness of enemies and to commend to the nations as practical politics the search for cooperation and peace"; and, that in a world of plenty the suffering of those enslaved by poverty is "an intolerable violation of God's good creation."

As those reconciled to God in Christ Jesus, I'd preached and prayed that we are sent to be God's reconciling community in a fractured world. That's what reconciliation meant to me. For the member who was, as civil rights activist Fannie Lou Hamer famously said, "sick and tired of being sick and tired," that open-ended hope didn't cut it in the here and now. She viewed talk of reconciliation not through a theological lens but as just another form of cheap, shallow kumbaya that put off into the undefined future the hard work of repair in race relations. For her, as the oft-cited quote goes, "justice delayed was justice denied." Years later, I better comprehend her pain and desperation.

OUT OF ORDER?

For that Caldwell member, for me, and for any church that seeks diversity and justice-centered life, Jennifer Harvey offers an important word. It may be, however, a slap in the face to those who center the Reformed doctrine of reconciliation in Christ in their faith without seeing it from another angle.

In her book, *Dear White Christians: For Those Still Longing for Racial Reconciliation*, Harvey, an associate professor of religion at Drake University, argues a vast amount of work to date toward true racial equality is out of sequence. She calls out all who have been working to build more diverse churches through reconciliation and points to a different way forward:

> The fact that we have been working for interracial, multicultural, diverse, and just reconciled faith communities for some time and have yet to see almost any sustained movement toward realizing such communities is a powerful indictment of the adequacy of reconciliation. Moreover, our failure to have realized these communities should also command our attention and lead us to the insight that, perhaps, something different is required.[1]

Alternatively, churches striving for diversity must work

toward *reparations first*, before racial reconciliation can come about, she contends. Given that her book was published before the election of Donald Trump, her argument has gained even more credibility because of the division that has since deepened in America. This may, however, come as unwelcome or even jarring to those who have been doing justice work for some time. It raises the unsettling specter that past work has, indeed, failed and that something new, in which most of us are deeply inexperienced, is required:

> A reparations paradigm slows us down in our racial visions. It requires us to not move so quickly, given the actual situation in which race locates us right now—with its legacies of unaddressed violence, oppression, subjugation, and devastation for which those of us who have benefited have yet to apologize, let alone make meaningful repair—to presume that inter-racial relationships and beloved community are even possible. A reparations paradigm requires us to ask the question that seems unthinkable to many white Christians: that without repentance and repair having come prior, why would we even assume interracial relations to be desirable or beneficial to people of color?[2]

In fact, Harvey says, continued work toward reconciliation, absent repentance and repair, may do more harm in our diverse faith communities than good.

PAINFUL TRUTHS—PAST AND PRESENT

As part of this journey, Harvey writes, we must dwell in "painful truths" that are "potentially liberating and trans-formative for all of us."[3] Slowly, more churches are investigating the "painful truths" she mentions. Some are current and urgent. Others are historical, but still speaking.

At Caldwell, Harvey's admonition hits close to home. In the years immediately following the church's unexpected rebirth, the congregation, elected leadership, and staff focused intensely on rebooting the church. That meant setting in place our mission statement and guiding principles, creating a focus for mission and justice ministries, restarting Sunday school, building a nursery, reorganizing the committee structure, setting a budget, establishing stewardship patterns, and chasing water leaks and other long-ignored repairs around our old buildings. We were plenty busy trying to make a future for the place we had inherited and unwittingly drawing on what were, for most of us, familiar patterns of leadership, hierarchy, and governance.

Truth be told, however, we had been too busy looking forward to look back and learn more about Caldwell's history. Inadvertently, we had committed the sin of overlooking the past for the corner of Fifth and Park Streets and how it should inform our living now.

That changed when we celebrated Caldwell's centennial in 2012. Elder Beth Van Gorp, a quiet but deeply committed and piercingly insightful servant of the Lord, took on the task of reading one hundred years of session minutes and other historical documents. She presented this history to us over several Sundays during the centennial year, putting it in context of Charlotte's and the nation's history.

What might have been an overlooked notation in the session minutes rocked the congregation's sense of itself and its place. We learned the church had begun life as John Knox Presbyterian in 1912. Ten years later, a childless widow, Sallie Caldwell White, left $50,000 to the church to honor her parents, David and Edith Caldwell. That's $750,000 in today's dollars.

The session renamed the church Caldwell Memorial to honor the family in gratitude for the transformative gift. The funds were used in 1922 to build the classic sanctuary that has hosted worship ever since.

Who were the namesake Caldwells?

In short, as Beth revealed to us in worship one Sunday, they were the last generations of a slaveholding family that made its fortune on a plantation in the northern reaches of the county, bordered by the Catawba River. We now know the names of some of the enslaved: William, Umphrey, Plum, Cyrus, Phyllas, Caleb, Lethy, Hannah, Henery, Nancy, Custis, James, Sucry, and . . . Easter.

Silence gripped those in the pews as we listened to this "news." Slowly, we processed what was now *our* painful truth: money from the blood, sweat, toil, mistreatment, lives, and deaths of enslaved people paid to build the holy space where we gathered, across our diversity, to worship God.

Many, many Southern churches, as with almost all Southern institutions if one digs deep enough, have histories that entangle their identity with slavery. But this was *our* history.

The revelation didn't stop there. Historical records indicated that David Caldwell, the last owner-operator of the plantation, fathered several children with one of the enslaved women. That meant there was a branch of the Caldwell family with African American blood, a branch whose members, of course, did not receive one penny of the $50,000 in 1922 dollars that was left to Caldwell.

Our white members' emotions ranged from sadness to shame and embarrassment. For many of our Black members,

126

however, this wasn't news. We were learning what they had known, what shaped their lives all along. Maybe not the specifics of the Caldwells and their money, but the how the heavy drape of white supremacy covers all of the South's history. We were reminded again of the truth from William Faulkner's *Requiem for a Nun*, itself a story about discovery and redemption from past sin and evil, "The past is never dead. It's not even past."

Several years, later, Caldwell is still processing what this history means and what it mandates. The childless widow Sallie Caldwell White was the last of the direct white line of the Caldwell family that we can trace. We have identified only one family member of Caldwells of color branch and have begun a slow, sensitive conversation with him about how we may balance repair and reconciliation. We are exploring various ways to share this part of our history more broadly, to name plainly its truth and to honor the names and stories of those they enslaved.

Meanwhile, we had more work to do. We took a close, unblinking look at the Southern Presbyterian church's complicity, in Charlotte and elsewhere, in slavery. We studied how the church used Scripture to legitimize and sustain what's been called America's original sin. We have confessed in worship that the stain of that sin is seeped into the ground where we worship, that the blood of Black lives is present in the plaster and the stained-glass windows of our sanctuary.

The congregation no longer calls itself Caldwell "Memorial," just Caldwell Presbyterian. We've come to see this as a quiet way to honor the first Caldwell Presbyterian, a church begun by the freed enslaved people of the Caldwell family on a piece of land given by David Caldwell after Emancipation. It was one of many Black Presbyterian churches started in the region by the Northern branch of the denomination. As Southern Presbyterians stood by, most likely quietly resisting, Northern Presbyterians came to help build institutions of learning, healing, and worship across the South for the support and advancement of those who had been enslaved.

Caldwell's past with slavery is such a somber and deep truth that the congregation is still processing, praying, confessing, and asking God for guidance about our ongoing response.

As white nationalism spreads in America and abroad, as extrajudicial police shootings continue, and as African Americans labor under the structural, generational, and institutional legacies of slavery and the white supremacy embedded in our national DNA, it seems increasingly clear America has no quick fixes for its racial discord and unreconciled state. Nor, as Harvey notes, should it. However urgent this crisis of national conscience is, we may well have to work through generational change before the mind of the country shifts to understand and repent as it moves into its majority-minority future.

The same goes for the church with its even greater urgency to stand in the gap with Christ in these difficult times. In the meantime, we face the risk of doing irreparable harm to our nation without facing the need to repair head on—and not just for the sake of dialogue.

WHAT DOES REPAIR LOOK LIKE?

What, then, does Jennifer Harvey have in mind?

What she doesn't propose is a long exploration about the payout of money. That's an important conversation, one that helps newcomers to the issue by putting the harm done in perspective in terms of dollars and cents.

Instead, though, Harvey focuses on structures and systems that harm people of color disproportionately by allowing white supremacy to persist, however subtly. First, she writes, more churches, but especially diverse churches, should focus more on the realities and problems of whiteness, which is a mindset of unearned privilege more than an issue of skin color. That includes understanding how race emerged as a social construct imposed over centuries by white people of power.

Arriving at this truth rejects what Harvey calls "abstract concepts" that cloud conversations and delay actions regarding race. It turns us "toward concretely engaging the material realities that mediate and alienate our interracial relationships."[4] She advocates three foci—"race as a social construct, an emphasis on particularity, and a focus on the repair of unjust structures."[5] Some of her examples of specific actions are:

- Acknowledge all Americans occupy what she calls "blood-soaked land" that was taken from America's first people.
- Engage concretely in helping immigrants who have fled untenable situations, including more compassionate reform of immigration laws and policies. Remember the Bible's command that we "welcome the stranger."
- Work to reform criminal justice and mass incarceration, both of which are irrefutably biased against people of color. I note this is an issue that attracts disciples of both conservative and progressive stripes.

- Intensify our actions to reverse the damage we are doing to the climate as stewards of God's creation.

As opposed to destructive acrimony, Harvey calls this work to repair what is broken in race relations "constructionism." It enables immediate engagement and can lead to tangible progress. She urges white people to be about this work without further burdening people of color to continue to explain why it is needed.

To be sufficient, this work "would relentlessly focus whites more on white supremacy and less on people of color."[6] And, soberly, she reminds us this work never ends:

> Thus, repair is the work. It is a constant and unending work. But while saying so may risk involving a process that sounds so overwhelming it includes despair, such framing radically reconfigures notions of relationality and justice away from a reconciliation paradigm that has proven endlessly unsatisfying. Such framing moves us from the inefficacious abstract toward concrete possibilities, hopeful possibilities.[7]

CAN THERE BE BOTH/AND, RECONCILING WHILE REPAIRING?

In the end, Harvey arrives where Kim and Shaw, authors of *Intersectional Theology*, land as well. That to be a truly diverse church, one I label as aspiring to be intersectional for a new America, congregations must become part of the resistance.

Where needed, white people must put their fragility aside and engage not just in candid conversation but real repair and restorative justice that deconstructs the white supremacy built into so many of the nation's systems and institutions. After twelve years as pastor to an intersectional faith community, my personal experience confirms Harvey's instinct that focusing on reconciliation alone gravely risks further damage to race relations as an incomplete, uncommitted, hollow, cheap way out.

After its brush with death, Caldwell's rebirth was shaped by a dream of racial reconciliation, perhaps one Harvey would call naive and ill founded. But, for us, it has been sincere, meaningful and transformational. As the resurrected Caldwell has lived out of the tomb as a "new thing," we have formed a new community of faith unlike any most of us have known.

In the meantime, through the lens of our faith, we have watched and processed together the sweeping changes in our nation and our city. We have rejoiced at the broader inclusion of the LGBTQ community, but we have had to battle efforts by the North Carolina General Assembly to reverse that progress. We have seen a deeply alarming counterreaction to President Obama's presidency in the once-unimaginable election of Donald Trump and how millions, from Congress to Main Street, have aligned devotedly behind what he represents.

Sharing these struggles, processing them together, and turning to the prophets' wisdom and the gospel of Christ's call for something different, the members of Caldwell are learning more and more about how to be vulnerable to each other as we talk about race. It has been murky, messy, and sometimes hurtful. We have made mistakes. I have made mistakes and hurt people inadvertently, and I have been made aware of my blunders in pointed but gracious ways.

A Lesson in Grace and Truth Telling in Love

As with many churches, each year at Caldwell we place a wooden cross on the front lawn to mark the season of Lent that leads to Easter, our highest and holiest day. One of the most moving services of the year comes on Maundy Thursday as we break bread in the way the apostles did and read the Scriptures recounting Christ's arrest, trial, and crucifixion. At the end of the service, we move to the cross outside and hang on it a black drape to mark the Triduum, remembering the three days Christ was in the tomb before his resurrection.

One Easter, I should have prepared far more than I did. I'd participated in a sunrise service in Uptown Charlotte and come back to the office to polish off my Easter sermon. I helped as I could with the Easter breakfast and watched as our members decorated the bare cross with fresh-cut spring flowers, giving it life to mark the resurrection. One of the best parts of this is seeing how our kids, dressed in a carefully chosen Easter outfit, love to pitch in. For children of all ages, it's a formative way to celebrate our new life in Christ.

In worship, when it came time for me to do the children's sermon, I wanted to explain what the flowers on the cross stood for, since so many of our kids had helped and since we had several new families with us that day. I showed them the plain, black drape that had hung on the cross for three days until that morning, when a ten-foot bouquet that wrapped the cross from bottom to top replaced it. I was winging it a bit and I chose my words carelessly. "Look at this ugly black cloth. Aren't all the flowers that God gives us in springtime—the ones you helped put on the cross—so much more beautiful?" Some members say they heard my voice catch as

I stumbled on the word "ugly," but it's what came out. It was Easter. There was so much more to do before the day would be over.

A few weeks later, an African American elder and I were driving back from a weekend session retreat. It was a good time to invite feedback and hear her thoughts. She had some—and I needed to hear them. She recalled how, on that Easter, another Black member of the church had come to her very upset about my terrible choice of words and what it said to any people of color in the packed church that day. She gently but clearly let me know the hurt I'd inadvertently caused, but said she had reassured the other Black member I had not intended at all to hurt anyone. I just made a thoughtless—but still damaging—mistake. I didn't deserve her grace.

That elder and I still don't always see everything the same, nor should we. But her viewpoint is one I look for when important matters are being discussed. As with God's grace, I had not earned her gentle treatment. If anything, I'd risked whatever trust I'd built with our members of color, especially our Black members. That elder still holds me accountable and for that I will always be profoundly grateful. She taught me more than she might know about truth and reconciliation and she is still teaching me.

As I observe life at Caldwell, through the ups and downs of our sometimes-precarious journey together across our differences, God continues to show me reconciliation is not about some singular moment. Rather, it's about everyday grace and truth telling in love, even when we make big mistakes.

BOTH/AND REPAIR
AND RECONCILIATION?

What about a both/and way forward—reconciliation while and through repair?

Charlotte prides itself as a "world-class" city, with its banking headquarters and as the recipient of many recent "best places to live" types of awards. Despite periodic recessions and slowdowns, the city has sustained a long-term upward trajectory spanning decade after decade. The landscape in certain parts of town prove it. Charlotte is teeming with millennials. They come to work for the banks, long one of Charlotte's bedrock industries, along with health care and entrepreneurial start-ups. New jobs are growing in "fintech" roles that combine technology and financial services, as well as other technology-related opportunities. Charlotte's light rail transportation, which reaches some but not all neighborhoods and socioeconomic levels of our city, has spurred years of explosive growth in apartment construction. The new city seal may feature young adults at breweries with dogs and scooters.

But then there is the other Charlotte. This sparkling city looks like Oz from the movies when the Goodyear blimp flies over with its cameras on Monday Night Football. But behind the sheen, we are and have long been two cities—one of haves and one of have-nots, a gap that inescapably follows racial lines between Black, brown, and white, a gap that risks becoming even deeper as fallout from the COVID-19 pandemic continues.

That truth became unavoidable in 2014 when nationally recognized researcher and thought leader Raj Chetty outed us. In a report through Harvard University, he and others presented data showing Charlotte ranked last among fifty cities and ninety-nine among one hundred counties in upward economic mobility. If one is born into poverty in Charlotte, it is harder than almost anywhere else in America to escape that poverty.

To the surprise and dismay of the city's business and chamber of commerce leaders, Charlotte's bottom ranking placed it in close company with Baltimore, a city many would think of long before our beloved town in terms of race- and poverty-related struggles, unfairly it proves. Immediately, the city launched efforts to study the results and the reasons behind them. A range of voices demanded real repair, not whitewash or wallpaper solutions.

But before any major strategies, initiatives, or responses surfaced, the city received an even more unmistakable signal that it had a race problem. In September 2016, Keith Lamont Scott, an African American, was shot and killed by police. The pot that had simmered quietly and, to many, imperceptibly finally boiled over. For four nights, Charlotte was the feature story on twenty-four-hour news stations as protestors marched the Uptown streets. It was a scene the city's elite could never have imagined and a second, big black eye to the face of Charlotte. Not here. Not this city. Not our streets. Not for four nights on CNN.

As one among thousands who walked many miles that week, including many faith leaders, I witnessed mostly peaceful protest, and I heard many bridge-building conversations among those who marched. Tragically, however, on the first night, protestor Justin Carr was shot and killed on the doorstep of a fancy Uptown hotel as protestors and police faced off. A local man was later found guilty of his murder, though pastoral colleagues of mine who were just feet away from that gunshot still have questions about where it originated.

On another night, a few glass windows on the ground floors of Uptown office buildings were broken. To some, it was a "riot." Others used far more accurate and reasonable terms like "protest" or "uprising." I marched with all kinds of people over several nights. I got close enough to tear gas to know that it's serious business. At times, I stood between ranks of police in riot gear and the protestors. Nothing happened.

But the gathering of armed forces "just in case" was ominous.

As we marched Uptown, we saw National Guard soldiers, called up by the governor, stationed in the first-floor garages under the glass-skinned skyscrapers that soared above the fray. One night, a relatively small group of protestors, the main body that was active that night, made it to my own neighborhood and passed by my front door. They were followed by two busloads of police "just in case."

As much as the Chetty economic mobility study, that week changed Charlotte forever. And it mobilized people of faith. It became a touchstone that still anchors dialogues about whether our city has made progress. Over the years to come, various stakeholders launched initiatives aimed at affordable housing, community development, public education, more widely available preschool, and support for Black-owned businesses.

By May of 2020, Charlotte was still a tale of two cities—one mostly white and prospering and the other mostly Black and still struggling. Just after Pentecost Sunday that year, a mighty wind blew across Charlotte, the nation, and the world when yet another unarmed Black person died at the hands of police. With the knee of a Minneapolis police officer pressed down on his neck for 8 minutes and 46 seconds, George Floyd fought for life, choking out the words "I can't breathe" until he breathed his last.

The nation exploded. A blend of righteous anger and awakening erupted into a wave of protests in dozens of US cities. For more than a week, citizens of all ages and races marched day and night chanting "Black Lives Matter!" and "This is what democracy looks like." Police in multiple cities fanned the flames of indignation over police brutality as they overreacted, using unnecessary force, highly militarized tactics, tear gas, and other means to suppress mostly peaceful protests. Then the fire spread worldwide as other nations made their own expressions of how Black Lives Matter through peaceful protests and community organizing.

In Charlotte, with the social fabric still torn from Keith Lamont Scott's killing in 2016, an unprecedented web of people of all faiths came together. Evangelicals acknowledged their own complacency and complicity in racial injustice at a major rally in an Uptown park, despite COVID-19 restrictions. Charlotte mayor Vi Lyles called me and others to rally the city's clergy to be on the streets to help keep the protests peaceful. Over the following week, as in 2016, I found myself walking miles and miles on streets (and at times, the interstate), sometimes standing between police in riot gear and young people trying to be heard.

When the Charlotte-Mecklenburg Police Department corralled and gassed peaceful protestors on the night of June 2, 2020, including Caldwell's youth minister Rev. Justin Martin, the same clergy leaders who had been called to help keep the peace quickly coalesced and called city officials to account. Alongside clergy of all kinds, I found myself among the leaders of a renewed push to review police policies, methods, and tactics. Police quickly changed tactics to give the peaceful protestors more room, and a spirit of community grew over several nights as more and more people added their voices. Without the pressure of looming police, protesters self-organized and the nightly demonstrations of solidarity became a beautiful witness to healthy and loving community.

Meanwhile, across the nation, signs of a new fusion movement began to emerge as a diverse mix of Americans kept up the protests for weeks. Fueled especially by a generation that grew up since Trayvon Martin's slaying, the energy spread from urban downtown areas to white suburban neighborhoods and then to small cities and towns in what the *New York Times* called "a glorious poetic rage" that many hoped and prayed would be a tipping point in the national consciousness related to police brutality and the valuing of Black lives.[8]

From Keith Lamont Scott's death in Charlotte in 2016 to the movement launched by George Floyd's lynching in 2020 and beyond, Caldwell continued to grow, learn, and refine its focus on justice. Through the Poor People's Campaign: A National Call for a Moral Revival, led by Rev. William Barber, Caldwell members had stepped up to practice civil disobedience in protest of the North Carolina General Assembly. We also examined and confessed the truth of whiteness. We invited an even wider range of speakers and preachers to bring their perspectives from the margins, especially to those of us who had for so long viewed how our city works from seats of comfort and privilege.

As an intersectional congregation, we have listened to voices within the church who side with Jennifer Harvey on her point about putting reparations before reconciliation. We weigh that with the promise of the words "in Christ" in Galatians 3:27–28 and how they offer a new order for God's

138

people, a liberation in how relationships can be formed that balance love and justice.

It's been said that justice is what love looks like in public, and our journey of learning repentance and action continues. We are, I believe, keeping Harvey's warning about moving too quickly toward declaring reconciliation close in mind. We work every day to understand what it means to move with urgency and with intentionality at once. We are moving more slowly and deliberately in our assessment of how we use our human, financial, and social capital. We remind ourselves to quiet the voices of traditional power and privilege so other voices among us can be heard. In 2020, the congregation declared its commitment to becoming an anti-racist congregation, as opposed to simply a missional, diverse one. This moved the church into a new season of even deeper reflection and action.

We are far from perfect. We still often stumble. We are on the journey along Harvey's reconciliation-reparations spectrum, asking God to guide us in leaning forward at all times and to recognize our blunders when they are pointed out to us by our minority leaders and members.

A particular blessing in this journey is the recent addition of a full-time associate pastor. Past associate pastors at Caldwell, each a woman of color, have been part of Caldwell's ministry for more than a decade, but their relationship was contractual as we built up our financial budget. In 2020, the congregation called Gail Henderson-Belsito as a full-time, called and installed associate pastor, a far more long-term commitment and promise of partnership. Deeply spiritual, gifted in preaching, and shaped by her own journey as an African American woman, Gail has brought enormous depth, compassion, strength, and passion to Caldwell's call to bear witness to God's love and justice in all it does.

PARTICULAR REPAIR?

Two more steps in closing: First, while we cannot say the idea originated with reparations in mind, we hope our dream of putting affordable housing on our church campus will advance our journey toward repairing what we can in our city. The ugly side of Charlotte's booming economy is we have a deep deficit of affordable places where the poor and working classes can live, lacking between 34,000 and 50,000 affordable units, according to various studies. Without a public-private response of unprecedented scale, Charlotte will not be affordable for those below middle class. As one journalist wrote, if one is a hotel housekeeper, a short-order cook, a landscaper, or anyone making $15 an hour or fewer, our city is showing anything but welcome.

With Harvey's emphasis on what she calls "particularity" in reparations in mind, we are aware Charlotte's affordable housing crisis hits mostly individuals and families of color. The potential economic shock waves of the COVID-19 pandemic will hit the most vulnerable the hardest. This includes families displaced by the urban renewal of the 1960s and 1970s, as well as those affected by the city's high rate of gentrification of its urban neighborhoods.

Caldwell envisions twenty-one apartments, as many as we have space for, occupied by a mix of people in poverty who are all living on or under 30 to 60 percent of the area median income. Perhaps it is the equivalent of the widow's mite against the enormity of a fifty-thousand-unit shortage. But it is what we can do.

So, we eagerly await the chance to welcome and embrace our new neighbors, some of whom will be in transition, others more long term. We intend to center the residents in shaping both the governance of the property and the nature of the living experience on campus. We intend to give the residents as much agency as we can as we work with the nonprofit organizations that will select the neighbors we hope will comprise a "beloved community," a mix of people affected by HIV/AIDS and others affected by disabilities. Caldwell's property will become theirs in part.

And it seems God has a way with numbers. We set a goal to raise an additional $600,000 in a congregational capital campaign to help pay for our housing dream. That fundraising campaign surpassed that goal and reached $750,000. That is the current equivalent of the $50,000 left to the church in 1922 from the Caldwell family's plantation fortune. To honor the people enslaved by the Caldwell family and the old South that shaped it, the congregation named the new apartment building "Easter's Home." The name recalls one of the enslaved people while also reminding us and our city of the hope we have as Easter people who are given second chances in Christ.

One can debate about whether this amounts to repair. As for the Caldwell community, however, the pursuit of this dream has advanced mutual understanding and deepened reconciliation in Christ across our members' differing races, classes, experiences, and backgrounds as they have worked together to bring it about.

AUDITING FOR JUSTICE

Another response has been to take a hard look at our portfolio of missions and justice efforts, including how we make financial grants in the city. After learning about the church's history with slavery, Caldwell members engaged in a weeks-long study on the difference between charity and justice. We're forever grateful to the two leaders who opened our eyes more widely in this study, Caldwell member Rev. Lori Thomas, a professor and program leader at the University of North Carolina at Charlotte, and Rev. Dr. Rodney Sadler, Old Testament professor and the head of Union Presbyterian Seminary's Center for Social Justice and Reconciliation. They continue to serve as advisors for all we do.

But we are listening to other voices as well. They speak from the walls of the 1922 sanctuary that was built with the money from the Caldwell Plantation. These voices are those of the enslaved people whose forced labor helped build the Caldwell fortune, part of which was left to the church.

These voices call us to act in the name of structural change—to work against any systems or institutions that protect or advance oppression, prejudice, inequality, and hate. So, we began examining everything we do in Christ's name for our neighbor. One could call it a "justice audit."

We are asking new questions of ourselves, such as: How do we understand our identity as servants of God? What are our personal motivations for getting involved in missions and justice work through the church? What perspectives of privilege do we bring to this work that may create blind spots for how we work with—and not for—those we seek to help? Are we aware of our biases and assumptions? Are we willing to listen and learn, to let go of old, ill-informed notions about the causes of our city's woes? Are we willing to be uncomfortable?

We are reassessing our partnerships with local agencies that fight hunger, poverty, homelessness, and other local challenges. With a bias toward social justice over charity, we are auditing every dollar we contribute to missions causes. We promise to educate ourselves about the root causes of local social challenges and how they can best be reversed for the long term.

We will assess our mission partners for how they treat their clients. Do they treat them as partners in the process of their rebound and recovery? Do their clients have a voice in the process? How do our partner agencies fit alongside others in our city's continuum of help and care?

Of ourselves, we are asking how we can do more to advocate for change in structures and institutions that tolerate or even feed inequality, injustice, and oppression. Are we as the body of Christ focused where needed on policy solutions? Are we leveraging our efforts ecumenically in effective ways? Are we willing to be physically present in the face of forces of hate and intimidation?

Yes, we still bring canned food on Sundays for the food bank. We make sandwiches for the hungry. On winter nights, we bring hot dinners and spend the night with our homeless neighbors at seasonal shelters. Those needs don't go away.

But in the meantime, we will keep listening to the voices in the walls of the sanctuary, the voices of those who did not have anyone to fight for them: William, Umphrey, Plum, Cyrus, Phyllas, Caleb, Lethy, Hannah, Henery, Nancy, Custis, James, Sucry, and Easter.

We pray they continue to talk to us—and that, as people of faith, we have ears to listen.

POSSIBILITIES AND POTENTIAL PITFALLS

Embodying Christ across diversity has never been easy or for the faint hearted, nor has it been reflected in success in large numbers. That's as true in the PC(USA) as it is in most mainline Protestant denominations. Multicultural churches, those who've focused on multiracial and multi-ethnic diversity, know the triumphs and trials that come with diverse membership. Intersectional churches that add diversity of class and LGBTQ identity know as well. Intersectional churches share a combination of distinct blessings and opportunities, offering a new way forward for the mainline Protestant church as America moves toward its inclusive, LGBTQ-valuing, majority-minority future.

But they also know tensions and distinct types of conflict (historical, if not current) tied to their diversity. Their experiences reflect our own at Caldwell as being gloriously messy. Sometimes it is pure glory, sometimes it is very messy, and most days it is a mix of both. But it's never dull. It is always life-giving, and Jesus has a way of showing up.

This chapter draws on the experience of intersectional congregations to provide a glimpse of the possibilities and potential pitfalls of congregations as they may one day be intersectional. None of this is comfortable or familiar to those of us who live in the majority and have known only "traditional," homogeneous church communities shaped largely by whiteness. Majority-white churches seeking deeper diversity should understand what will be required of their white members, no matter how committed on paper they are.

Intersectional churches are called to resist the idea that the mainline Protestant church can remain about 90 percent white—in the PC(USA)'s case—and keep what diversity it has mostly in silos and swim lanes, people of color worshipping at some churches and white folks at others. True integration across color, class, sexual orientation, and gender diversity comes with and through members' commitment to welcoming the wounded and the outsider. This resistance requires constantly practicing to center voices that were once on the outside, which brings both organizational complexity and fragility.

In their 2003 article in *Sociology of Religion*, Brad Christerson and Michael Emerson draw on a range of research and their own study of a diverse congregation to document and explore reasons for the underlying fragility of diverse congregations. They find a differing experience among members in the minority racial/ethnic group in contrast to members in the majority.

Majority members largely experience benefits (their needs are easily met by same race members, so the addition of "diversity" is experienced largely as an additional positive to the congregation), whereas minority members experience both costs and benefits. (They

146

venture across racial boundaries not just for enjoyment and novelty, but to gain meaning and belonging, which entails more effort and more risk.)[1]

For example, what types of churches and church backgrounds come into the new mix can bring both blessings and potential trip wires. For most members, church polity and governance are out of sight and mind until it is needed, often amid tension and conflict. Polity and governance may be included in new members' classes, but that often goes mostly forgotten. How polity and governance are practiced in the hands of leaders forms a touchstone either for healing or division.

While the intersectional churches I studied tend to be more relaxed in their use of polity and doctrine, the rules do matter at times. If members understand them differently, confusion and disappointment find oxygen.

Christerson and Emerson add, "The costs of being a minority member of a multiethnic congregation will be greatest, it would seem, for those with religious histories that differ the most from the majority group."[2]

Churches often cite how, in the early days of the Jesus movement, the apostles owned everything "in common."[3] Often they are referring to material things such as money. Sometimes overlooked is the prior sentence, which says, "All the believers were of one heart and soul." One way to "hold all things in common," is for individual members to give to their church and for their church to write checks to nonprofit organizations and justice-related partners that do the "missions" work. More difficult, especially for the majority, is the work of building a community that is one in heart and mind across those gaps, committing to quiet one's own experience or perspective to hear and honor the other in relational, empathy-deepening community.

As he closed his letter to the Galatians, Paul called on them to "bear one another's burdens."[4] The possibilities that accompany being an intersectional church soar when those in the majority are quick to hold their tongues, quiet their privilege, and listen first. Intersectional communities reach their full potential in Christ when the members of one oppressed group enter into the experience and suffering of another group. Importantly, as Emmanuel Lartey notes, this requires particular awareness, training, and sensitivity to embrace the other's perspective, not just for clergy and staff, but also for as many members as possible.

"Intercultural pastoral care has to be a corporate, cooperative activity in which the *many* work together for *each* and for *all*," Lartey writes. "Practitioners of pastoral care have to be aware of the symbols and signs present in different cultures and be willing to learn from each other about what caring for persons might mean in different contexts."[5]

It takes courage, stamina, and emotional fortitude, even from the most committed. As important, it calls for churches and their leaders to follow Christ to the margins and to rethink many aspects of community, service, worship, and, yes, occasional disagreement or conflict. Before a recent revision, the PC(USA)'s constitution, the Book of Order, called churches to "risk their lives for the sake of the gospel." We mainliners need to get a lot more comfortable with taking risk, naming and checking our power and privilege, and trusting God.

As Kujawa-Holbrook and Montagno write: "To be sure, models of pastoral care that take seriously love and power are risky."[6]

BLESSINGS FROM DIVERSITY

Asked to name their blessings from diversity, intersectional church pastors spoke out of abundance:

- Diversity "strengthens and facilitates a healthy evangelism. . . . Visitors see the diversity in our pews and pastoral leadership and are drawn to learn more about the church and consider membership. Also, the diversity of the church adds a vibrancy to all our discussions around mission." —First Presbyterian, Brooklyn

- "There is an unquantifiable feeling of welcome and openness felt by both black and white members and visitors. . . . Our church isn't conceivable without (its diversity). The desire for diversity and new ways of belonging motivated the creation of this church. Dealing with successes and failures in regard to this aspect of things has shaped us." —Durham Presbyterian, Durham

- "There is a great energy in all the events that I believe comes, in part, from the way the congregation sees itself as a diverse community. Also, we have some interesting programs, perspectives, and resources we may not otherwise have." —Jefferson Avenue Presbyterian, Detroit

- "Diversity in our congregation blesses us by its witness to what's possible. LGBTQ leadership with hetero [cisgender, heterosexual] allies. Openness, forgiveness, and grace." —East Liberty Presbyterian, Pittsburgh

- "A diversity of experiences of God in and through a diversity of experiences in life. Different cultural backgrounds from foods brought to potlucks to prayers shared in worship to conversations over mealtime. Great talents cultivated across a wide range of experiences all brought together both in how we make decisions and in the decisions we ultimately choose to make." —Brown Memorial Presbyterian, Baltimore

These congregations also know diversity takes many forms. It's multilayered and non-formulaic. At Oaklands Presbyterian in Laurel, Maryland, Rev. LeAnn Hodges points to differences in theological outlook rather than diversity of race/ethnicity, gender, class, or sexuality.

We have a gathering of people who embody the beloved community of God more than any other place in my life. This affords us the space to practice living in a way that the world does not teach us. We learn empathy and perspective. Second, we have created a culture that strives for balance, where the "opposing side" actually brings out the best in the other. The "progressive" end of the continuum has the drive for social justice and an intellectual and compassionate approach to Scripture. The shadow of this group is that they can be overly elitist and can become so enamored by thoughts and ideas that there is little passion in the expression of their faith. The "conservative" end of the continuum is all about the passion and are well versed in Scripture. Its shadow is that they can be overly moralistic, chaotic, and more comfortable living with moralistic absolutes.

Sometimes, congregation and community aren't the same thing, adds Brown Memorial's Rev. Andrew Foster Connors:

> Our congregation is actually more diverse in our worship attendance than in our formal membership. We see more and more people who designate themselves as "going to Brown Memorial" without actually joining the church. . . . I believe that people seek out our church and its witness because of the foundational commitment to diversity. This is seen in our Facebook presence—with six hundred more "friends" on Facebook than we even have members.

Several of these churches are "destination churches." Their members drive past many other, more conventional and convenient, churches to attend worship and other offerings. This reflects our experience at Caldwell. Members of our faith community hail from twenty-five zip codes, four counties, and two states (Charlotte is on the border of the Carolinas). A geographic spread like that, as opposed to being a true neighborhood church, means some traditional programming, such as weekly Wednesday night dinner and learning that are within a convenient drive for most members, are less likely to succeed. Members' lives are busy, and the longer distances to drive, often in crowded urban areas, works against some mainstay programming familiar to traditional churches.

Current worship attendance trend data define "regular" attendance in worship as once or, maybe, twice a month. That's especially true for "destination churches." They must work harder through other means of community and communications to keep more-scattered flocks aware of events and plugged in to what's happening. Even with smaller budgets, intersectional congregations were often savvy in the use of online communications before the pandemic. Now many, including Caldwell, have discovered online community can be a powerful means of broadening and strengthening community. Caldwell, for example, added new vespers and other classes online during the pandemic's stay-at-home orders. The pandemic also accelerated how we offer our regular worship service online each week, broadening the regular Caldwell community well beyond Charlotte.

At the same time, inclusive churches keep in mind that some members, because of age or socioeconomic reasons, are not as online as often, if at all. In Caldwell's case, during the pandemic, we paired each member needing a little tech help with a "tech buddy" to help iron out any challenges. But, to be sure, we do not see online gatherings as a substitute for the warmth and connection of in-person classes and programs. They are, instead, a supplement.

In addition, their diversity shapes these churches' outreach, helping them guard against patriarchal blind spots. "The [congregation's] varied experiences help us to consider our responses to community needs from an eye-level, collegial perspective" as opposed to a privileged, top-down model, explains Rev. Randy Bush at East Liberty Presbyterian. "We engage with others more as peers than as benevolent benefactors. Also, when outside groups or visitors connect with our church, the diversity causes them to adjust their preconceived ideas, such as, 'Oh, you must be a rich, white church given the size of your building,' and adjust their assumptions when they see leaders and participants from a wide range of social groups."

To have diversity of thought in decision-making requires having not just diverse members but also diverse lay leaders.

Bush adds that leadership development is an intentional and primary focus, given the nuances in leading across diversity:

> We are intentional to invite a diversity of people so that a great number of trained people are in the pipeline to be tapped in the future and so that we have a more informed community. Externally, it shows up in the diversity of our mission partners and social outreach. It is not without its challenges. There is an expectation that we will respond to everything but that is not sustainable. We are working now to fine tune what specifically we are called to do and be in the world in the midst of our diversity.

That be-all-things-to-all-people dynamic slips in at other churches as well. "Everyone has their own idea of what we should do and why," says Rev. LeAnn Hodges of Oaklands Presbyterian. "If we embraced everyone's ideas as a congregation, we would get nothing done. Instead, we have moved to commission members to work 'in their field.' . . . but we only embrace a mission initiative in the congregation if there is a sense of a larger group of people who are ready to champion that.

"Diversity in thought, background, race, and culture also produces the need to balance the goals of evangelism and new member outreach," Hodges concluded.

"We are all over the place! Our fastest growing demographic for a while was our African membership, who are adept at evangelism," she said. "As that became apparent, we realized that our African members had a lot to teach us about embracing an invitational ministry.

"If we wanted to maintain a diverse community, then we all had to be intentional about being inviting and welcoming. Interestingly enough, the demographic that grew as a result of a broader scope of evangelism was our LGBTQ members, and now there is a greater balance of our diversity in each new members' class."

TENSION WITH A TWIST

No church is without conflict, at least for very long. Conflict in diverse and intersectional churches has its own flavor. As diverse backgrounds, experiences, interests, passions, and opinions gather, disagreement is inevitable. Intersectional churches require a special measure of skill and perspective to navigate disagreement and keep community together. There is no shortage of what can spark disagreement.

At Durham Presbyterian, its energetic pursuit of justice and diversity at once opens the doors to a range of tensions, noted Rev. Franklin Golden:

> Oh boy, where to begin? Conflict over where attention is given: African American members or covenant relationship with our sister Hispanic congregation? Conflict over leadership styles, music, how to talk about reconciliation vs. justice. Conflict when a group of people who are more sophisticated about race stuff end up alienated from the rest of the church. Conflict when a black man cries out for help and no one responds because they are scared. . . . Less conflict lately, in part, because we are less diverse, but also because there is more trust. We've been through some stuff and navigate new challenges easier.

At intersectional churches, where challenging the status quo is the norm, congregations live in what I have come to call at Caldwell "constructive tension." The idea of tension tends to be viewed as a negative. But in these churches, constructive tension can generate positive energy, awareness, activity, and focus that advance empathy, understanding, and progress. As with a taut guitar string, constructive tension can sound beautiful notes. It results when everyone believes their voice matters. Constructive tension can also make church life messy and exhausting, as Pittsburgh's East Liberty Presbyterian's Rev. Randy Bush knows:

> Conflict arises when people feel we are not welcoming enough to political conservatives or when we are not more nuanced in some of the stances we take regarding sexual identity, racism, or immigration policies. However, people also recognize we are [as] outspoken as we are because we are naming the issues/concerns of the diverse populations in our pews. If diversity is to be valued, then the dominant cultural narrative has to be challenged/questioned through the sharing of others' experiences.

He continues:

> Occasionally, new African American/international members of our church have trouble accepting our stance on LGBTQ inclusion. Also, people coming from more conservative churches wonder about our Biblical hermeneutics—e.g., how come their prior churches always said "X" while we always say "Y." Lastly, there is frequently a tension between celebrating the gifts of a particular group and yet worrying that doing so will feel elitist and cause others to feel left out. All three of these concerns can be navigated, but it takes some pastoral sensitivity and organizational flexibility.

At Brown Memorial, Baltimore, its deepening diversity brings the same richness and complications, adds Rev. Andrew Foster Connors:

> The more diverse we become, the more challenges we face in engaging each other openly around social location. In one week, I had the resignation letter from two white gay men who said we were making white people "feel guilty" for talking about white supremacy, and the session had a letter from someone else angry that we had not acted on our inclusive values by hiring a part-time employee who is another white man. Talking about race is a great gift, but it's also a challenge to engage each other across an ancient divide that continues to operate in strong ways in our world, including the church.

Rev. LeAnn Hodges of Oaklands Presbyterian cited the challenge of creating "the space to invite new leaders who are conditioned to be on the outside looking in ... especially in a congregation with the history of being a pastor-centric congregation. It is about taking a lot of baby steps of invitation, listening, adapting, compromising."

Hodges noted another potential area of tension from diversity comes out of disagreement in biblical interpretation "relative to the congregation's embrace of LGBTQ people from some of our African members." Indeed, as mainline Protestant churches seek opportunities to welcome members from South and Central America and Africa, they are likely to encounter more conservative interpretations of what Scripture says about sexuality.

A particular danger point and fertile ground for disagreement at any church is a change in pastoral leadership, all the more so in intersectional congregations that mix a range of members' expectations and hopes, often flavored by their past wounds and unresolved pain from conflict at other churches. These intersectional congregations put a great deal of weight on the race, gender, sexuality, and other qualities of their pastoral leadership. That can create opportunities for disagreement and disappointment when, inevitably, a broadly mixed and diverse set of hopes cannot ever be completely fulfilled in any clergy change. But conflict can also strengthen congregations that make it through to healing on the other end, as First Brooklyn's Rev. Adriene Thorne described:

> It took the congregation ten years between the last installed pastor and me. A lot of that transition was conflict related to diversity. Was an African American pastor the answer? Was a male or female? Was someone racist if they liked a particular candidate and not some other? Did people really know each other after worshipping together for decades if they couldn't agree on the same pick? Members left the church. Folks are still healing. And conversations were had that makes this one of the healthiest communities I have ever been a part of. They got a lot of stuff on the table. It's not perfect, but it's good.

CONFLICT COMES TO CALDWELL

The season came for Caldwell to learn the same lesson.

To live out of its commitment to diversity, the congregation added a second ordained pastoral leadership role with the commitment that it be held by a person of color. To be a diverse congregation, members and visitors must have pastoral leadership that reflects more than just one experience.

In our case, that was mine. But members and visitors needed to experience what diversity brings to worship leadership, pastoral care, preaching, teaching, and visioning.

After its resurrection, Caldwell added a second pastoral position as soon as it was financially feasible, though the church's financial footing was by no means guaranteed. To be fair to the person in the new position, Caldwell could only offer the role on the basis of an annual contract, rather than an installed or permanent position, because of the budget's unpredictability in those early years. Following Presbyterian governance, the position would be classified as "temporary."

The first person to be the temporary associate pastor, a woman of color, was well loved, succeeded, and retired at age sixty-seven. Years later, the session faced a hard decision, months in the making, not to renew the contract of the second person to hold the role, also a woman of color. Only the session had the full rationale, which it kept confidential as a personnel matter in fairness and professionalism to all. The session knew it would be difficult news for some and thoughtfully prepared to present the decision as transparently and sensitively as possible.

But unanticipated external events made the timing terrible. The announcement came in the same week as the tragedy at "Mother" Emanuel African Methodist Episcopal Church in Charleston, South Carolina, where white supremacist Dylann Roof gunned down nine Black members. The convergence of events, the Charleston tragedy, and the session's decision hit a nerve with some members. Some African Americans members strongly felt the session had been unfair in making the decision and unkind in its handling. Other Black members understood the reasoning and supported the session. A few white members sided with the Black members who disagreed. In the days and weeks that followed, private meetings were held. Names were called and rumors spread. I was verbally attacked, as were members of the session.

Anyone who has experienced church conflict knows this experience and its pain on all sides. But our conflict had particular dynamics due to Caldwell's diverse membership and mission. Call it a honeymoon or something else, but some members had come to believe Caldwell could or should have been able to avoid all conflict. Members voiced differing management and leadership philosophies. A few members said they believed a church should never terminate the employment of anyone but always find an alternative way forward. Having tried to live by these ideals, members who were disappointed felt the conflict all the more deeply. Disillusion in leadership and the pierced hope of the "ideal" church shattered some members' dreams and, in turn, their comfort in church or other members.

In some ways, these experiences echo conflict and tension at any church. But this conflict had a distinct intersectional aspect to it. After angry and hateful words had been hurled at them at other churches, many LGBTQ members had come to think of Caldwell as a safe space. When hurt feelings broke out, members who were still healing from conflict elsewhere began to stay away from worship. Some didn't return, but most did. In the end, about ten members, including Black and white, LGBTQ and straight, left the church during or after the time of tension. That may sound like a small number, and financially and missionally, the church did stay on track. Still, the congregation felt the conflict's impact, some more than others, for at least a year. Those on all sides of the conflict learned invaluable lessons. Everyone did their best to examine ourselves, see and confess our sins, and admit our failures, whether intended or not. Over time, relationships have healed, and we all know much more about the complexity of what we are striving to do.

Two years later, several Caldwell members reflected on that season in the church's life. Kim Bohannon, a white woman and gay elder, drew parallels to family. "It's like a family—and that can be a blessing and bring its challenges," she said. "Like any family, we love. We hug. We nurture and we have compassion toward one another. But at the same time, we have challenges just like any family has. We have conflict. We disagree. We argue. We hurt each other's feelings and we struggle to forgive. But in the end, we are still a family, and families grow together, love one another, and struggle through the conflict to be better."

Elder Wilma Petty, a straight, Black woman on the session at the time, recalls the deep uncertainty about Caldwell's future that she felt amid the struggle, along with the presence of God throughout: "I was on the session and we had to make decisions. We knew those decisions, which were made in fairness and, given lots of time to consider, had to be done. But during that time, we lost members. That was very difficult and very painful, but God brought us through that, and we came through it stronger."

Elder Doreen Byrd, an African American woman, reminded us that sometimes no amount of good intention will erase some blind spots. What hangs in the balance—and may be the most critical thing before, during, and after a conflict—is trust, she said:

> One problem with being intersectional is that we walk into the situation viewing the world through our own lenses. But we can't truly understand what it's like to be somebody else. So, try as we might, that's going to

affect how we handle things. You can have a dozen things go right but the one that goes wrong seems to carry so much more weight because the scale wasn't balanced in the first place. One may start off with the view that certain people are not inclined to be fair or are going to pull power. So, it's hard to build trust and maintain it under those circumstances. We have people here who were rejected at other churches and that makes that trust all the more fragile.

Churches that aspire to diversity and intersectionality are well advised to understand how nuanced relationship building and relationship sustaining can be. Rev. Adriene Thorne at First Presbyterian in Brooklyn hits a cautionary note for all diverse congregations: "I would add that there were also a lot of unexamined assumptions. There are underlying needs and unexpressed pain."

Diverse churches that mix cultural practices, communication styles, and members' backgrounds in other denominations and church traditions should be aware the environment can be ripe for misunderstanding. "In most cases, conflict has emerged from a lack of understanding of what is driving the other and failure to grasp the others' understanding of what is 'normal,'" says Oaklands Presbyterian's Rev. LeAnn Hodges. "Often times, something that seems so obvious turns out to be far from it."

POLITY AND THE PRIMACY OF RELATIONSHIPS

As at Caldwell, almost all the churches said their "growing pains" resulted in a stronger, more cohesive congregation.

"We learned the importance of sticking together for the

long haul; diversity is never achieved or sustained by quick fixes," observed Rev. Randy Bush. "We have found value in spending intentional time together—talking during committee meetings, retreats, conferences, Bible studies. We've also learned . . . to build relationships over and over again."

At Oaklands, Rev. LeAnn Hodges adds: "It's all about listening deeply, being slow to judge, not assuming we understand the motives or drivers of another, and allowing space for missteps. We are learning how to have difficult conversations about what matters most deeply. And we tend to laugh a lot together. I think that helps."

First Presbyterian-Brooklyn's Adriene Thorne emphasizes longevity of effort when it comes to reconciliation across differences. "It requires consistency, especially when dealing with wounds that are deep. The biggest changes I see are when people refuse to back down from relationships and stick it out through hard feelings."

Another truth out of conflict is sometimes members and churches need to part ways. "Sometimes, reconciliation looks like letting people leave," said one pastor, echoing several.

At Capitol Heights, Denver, which has experienced differences over "the character and practice of social witness," Rev. Mark Meeks noted the congregation has learned "simply to respect diversity, which includes diversity of social witness, and bless people when disagreement occurs while still moving in an orientation to which the congregation as a body decides upon."

The Avenue's Rev. Floretta Watkins adds: "While I was in South Africa, I heard the phrase, 'It takes two banks to build a bridge.' That's my metaphor for reconciliation. That and truth telling."

POLITY, GOVERNANCE, AND COMMUNITY

One thing that differentiates mainline Protestant churches from other, newer traditions is polity that is rooted in history but striving to fit contemporary congregations. Mainline Protestant congregations trace their polity to a reformation five hundred years ago that highlighted timeless issues, such as a balance of power, representative leadership, and the danger of idols in any form. Most important, each looks to Jesus Christ as the head of the church.

In these days of social pluralism and emerging theologies, is church polity a help or a hindrance in fostering diversity, managing conflict, and achieving reconciliation? Opinions among the pastors at intersectional churches vary. In several instances, to correct historical imbalances of power and privilege, clergy focus on leadership models that seat power more in relationships than in rules.

"Our polity doesn't provide much except good theological background and resources. Too much of a focus on the nuts and bolts of polity has brought 'rules' to the forefront when what we need to privilege is relationships," Rev. Andrew Foster Connors observed.

At Oaklands, Rev. LeAnn Hodges sees mixed blessings in her tradition's polity. "Honestly, it has been a challenge more than help. Our ordered form of government and Robert's Rules of Order and committee structure seem overly sanitized for our younger members (mainly LGBTQ) and our African American members." In the next breath, she adds, "Our polity of checks and balances and empowerment of laity are two aspects I am working hard to model, and there seems to be a growing appreciation. But we have a way to go."

Several churches noted appreciation for how church polity balances group discernment with individual conviction. These pastors appreciate procedures for dialogue and community decision that, ideally, allow differences to surface and a consensus to form. In the words of one, "My sense is that our polity makes room for diversity but does not require it."

As Rev. Randy Bush at East Liberty adds, no contemporary circumstances, demographics, or demands should cloud who the church follows:

> The connectionalism at the heart of Presbyterian polity reminds us that we are all in this work together under the guidance and grace of Jesus Christ. Sadly, the predominant mindset and organizational style of Presbyterians today is far more congregational than connectional, thus making it hard to build our denomination's strengths in working for a more diverse church.

In conclusion, perhaps a final word about the possibilities and potential pitfalls of these churches aspiring to live out their intersectional diversity should be given to the apostle Paul. These congregations understand when he says, "If I must boast, I will boast of the things that show my weakness."[7] Why, because his weakness points to God's strength. In seeking to be the body of Christ across their many types of diversity, in surrendering the hierarchical patterns of leadership that have guided the church for so long, in naming and checking privilege, in centering those who are used to being on the outside looking in, these churches lay themselves bare. They cast aside illusions of their own strength and, in the doing, they expose the weakness inherent in any organization or leadership. At the same time, they come to see anew God's grace and mystery amid their risky, gloriously messy, and, sometimes, constructively tense lives together as Christ's body.

LESSONS LEARNED

God's church, in all of its forms, has been on a journey for two thousand years. The question is, "Who and what is it following?"

Fifteen years ago, the Presbytery of Charlotte (a regional governing body of PC(USA) congregations) followed logic, tradition, and demographic projections. Charlotte was founded by Presbyterians. In the 1980s, Presbyterians from one church made up two-thirds of the city council. The main roads are named for two-hundred-year old Presbyterian churches. Charlotte is also a business town, level headed and data driven. So, even in church matters, logic, tradition, and placing "safe bets" on demographic projections had always worked.

With church planting in mind, Presbytery leaders checked the same trend data that real estate developers used to plan new homes, apartments, and shopping centers. The safe bet for planting a new church was what's known in Charlotte as "the Wedge." For decades, affluence and prosperity had pushed southeast from the center city well past Caldwell and many other churches, defining a particular slice of Charlotte's pie. With each new ring of leafy suburbs and new schools, the Presbyterians started a new church to serve the upper-middle class white folks. Each time it had "worked" in the sense that the new church plant had thrived.

So, even as many historically Black congregations in other parts of the city struggled, the Presbytery invested a large sum of money in a piece of land in the exurbs in line with the Wedge's expansion southward. What the city needed was one more "tall-steeple" church in the outer suburbs, Presbytery leaders concluded.

"If you build it, they will come," said the voice they heard, as if they were in the Iowa cornfield from the movie *Field of Dreams*.

The response came back, "If you want to make God laugh, tell God your plans."

The Great Recession of 2007–2008 hit Charlotte hard. The economy locked up like an old motor that had run out of oil. Churches froze their budgets first, then started cutting. Some didn't survive the recession. With tens of thousands of dollars in debt service on the land acquisition now adding strain to the Presbytery budget, it wavered on the edge of financial ruin. Leaders made tough decisions to make drastic cuts to one of the largest Presbytery staffs in the country, leaving two people to serve about 120 churches at the time. The Presbytery eventually sold the land in the Wedge to get back on its feet, taking a loss of more than $1 million.

The magi didn't have demographic projections when they set out to meet the new king. They followed a star that led them not to an affluent "wedge" suburb of Bethlehem but to a lowly manger surrounded by livestock where a peasant couple held a newborn. Their revelation, their epiphany, was captured in these lyrics from a hymn of the Iona community:

I sought him dressed in finest clothes,
where money talks and status grows;
but power and wealth he never chose:
it seemed he lived in poverty.
I sought him in the safest place,
remote from crime or cheap disgrace;
but safety never knew his face:
it seemed he lived in jeopardy.
Then, in the streets, we heard the word
which seemed, for all the world, absurd:
that those who could no gifts afford
were entertaining Christ the Lord.
And so, distinct from all we'd planned,
among the poorest of the land,
we did what few might understand:
we touched God in a baby's hand.[1]

Surely the magi left liberated. Surely today's church needs a similar epiphany and liberation.

I share the story of the Charlotte Presbytery not to point fingers. I spent eighteen years at a global banking giant. I made plenty of leadership decisions there based on logic and cold calculations and, admittedly, saved too much of my faith for Sundays. But God is known to use far different criteria. If we are lucky, we get caught in the way.

The pastors and elders of the intersectional churches I discovered didn't invite the circumstances that led to their transformation. As with the magi, they set out following a star but stuck to the main roads, at least at first. But these congregations did, indeed, encounter poverty and jeopardy. For several, their once-affluent neighborhoods reversed course. There came the day when their leaders had to chart a different way forward. Which road are Protestant mainliners following today?

LESSONS ON THE WAY

Being or becoming an intersectional, justice-oriented, both/
and church is more art than science. But in the end, it is neither. It is a Spirit-led, Spirit-dependent venture for which
there is no roadmap or map app that calls out easy-to-follow
directions. It calls for humility, patience, grace, and the
courage to take the long view of what God is doing.

Each of the intersectional churches I have described left
the main road of church identity and mission decades ago.
Each charts its own course day by day, month by month,
and budget year by budget year. Each has its own story,
ministry context, urban circumstance, leadership, congregational mix, potential futures, and existing challenges. Each
knows the "glorious messiness" of what happens when
believers come together across differences, bringing their
joys and sorrows, wonder and wounds.

While becoming or remaining an intersectional church
resists a "five-easy-steps" approach, the wisdom of these
pastors and their congregations, along with our journey at
Caldwell, yield some clear lessons learned about a way forward, in whole or in part, for the broader mainline Protestant church. Here are a few.

THE POWER OF LIFE AFTER DEATH

Each of these congregations knows what it is to "die to one-
self" in one or multiple ways. They know the gift of new
possibilities and new life. Generational decline in membership, urban forces such as "white flight" to the suburbs,
and other factors left these congregations facing existential
questions: Would they close, merge with another congrega-

tion, move to the suburbs, or open themselves to become "a new thing?"

With the intervention of God, each chose to find a way forward by opening itself up to rebirth. As one pastor put it, many of these churches "grew small," shrinking numerically but growing in the richness and dynamism of their congregation's adjusted course. Affected by its city's decline to 600,000 people from more than one million, Brown Memorial Park Avenue, for example, chose to "begin a period of creative experimentation in worship alongside fearless commitment to social justice." In the case of Durham Presbyterian, the product of merged congregations, few expected the merger to succeed. Today, says Rev. Franklin Golden, "our life together isn't conceivable without" its diversity. Each received the gift of transformation that exceeds what their congregations knew to expect.

"We have a gathering of people who embody the beloved community of God more than any other place in my life," reflects Rev. LeAnn Hodges of Oaklands Presbyterian in Laurel, Maryland. "This affords us the space to practice living in a way that the world does not teach us."

LEADING-EDGE PRACTICES

Intersectional churches often live on the leading edge of new practices in worship, ministry, and leadership development. Perhaps because of their inherent openness and hunger for fresh expressions of their faith, these intersectional churches center themselves on justice and follow their diversity in multiple aspects of their lives together.

One of these congregations practices only traditional worship. The rest work hard to reflect the diversity of their congregations in diverse worship leadership, styles, and emerging practices. In missions and outreach, intersectional churches tend not to be top-down "program churches." Rather, they follow the interests of their members more organically, acknowledging this sometimes risks diluting their mission efforts and may spark disagreement along the way. These intersectional churches are missional in nature. Primarily externally focused rather than tending mostly to their own members, these congregations balance member care and nurture with their natural bias to care for the "oth-ered" neighbor. They rooted their identities in advocacy and activism long ago, leaving their buildings and grounds to seek the face of Jesus in the homeless, the hungry, and the powerless, as well as often finding it among their own mem-bers who suffer oppression or, as Christ said in the Beati-tudes, are spiritually poor in other ways.

These churches know that diverse, if not intersectional, churches call for new styles of leadership and leadership development rather than the traditional, top-down, hier-archical forms that denominational polity often produces. These newer practices ensure power and equity in congre-gational leadership are shaped to resist and reverse more established structures that perpetuate the exclusion or sup-pression of long-marginalized voices and opinions. They center the other and empower those who traditionally have been on the outside looking in.

THERE IS DIVERSITY WITHIN DIVERSITY

The more diverse the church, the more complex its life together. This statement may seem obvious, but it's an important fact for those who work for a more diverse, inter-sectional church. Congregations that seek diversity often look for it from all directions. Majority congregations that add one or two minority or marginalized populations have their own dynamics. Those woven from more strands of difference will present more complexity and possibility.

Rev. Andrew Foster Connors at Baltimore's Brown Memorial puts it: "The more diverse we become, the more challenges we face in engaging each other openly around social location."

That said, it should be noted most of these congregations seek greater diversity than they already count.

INCLUSION AND PROPHETIC WITNESS

Made up of members with wide interests, passions, and, often, above-average energy and engagement, these churches must work hard, straining at times, to balance varied desires for how the church should bear public witness and be the hands and feet of Christ in their communities. The risk of disappointing members who feel their issues get overlooked runs higher at these churches, in part because they tend to attract those who have been hurt by the church elsewhere in their lives. Pastoral maturity, sensitivity, and self-differentiation are critical skills in leadership, both lay and clergy.

Their pastors feel free to preach prophetically and take on the powers and principalities they see as opposed to God's vision for a just community. But several struggle to make a safe space for more politically or theologically conservative members—even as they feel called to disrupt the status quo in institutions and systems that continue to marginalize people of color, the LGBTQ community, and those in poverty.

Rather than polished member recruitment campaigns and targeted marketing strategies, these congregations practice public witness as evangelism. They are often in the streets or otherwise where the marginalized are under pressure, and they attract new members as a result. For example, Caldwell always sees an increase in visitors in the weeks that follow the annual Pride parade, in which we annually enter a float featuring our gospel choir and members march in groups of fifty or so. Many of those visitors, both LGTBQ and straight, join and become active disciples. Similarly, Caldwell and its choir participate in the annual parade honoring the Rev. Dr. Martin Luther King Jr.

THE TOUCHSTONE OF PASTORAL LEADERSHIP, ESPECIALLY IN TRANSITION

At least half of the congregations I studied endured deep, bitter, and, in some cases, lasting conflict as they called new pastoral leadership. They emerged stronger and more tightly knit but not without loss and pain. In several cases, congregations and their leadership found conflict was rooted in the nuances of understanding across cultures, church traditions, and even language that are so essential in diverse communities. "Unwritten rules" and different ideas of what is "normal" in church governance that were assumed and obvious to some were not so obvious or understood by others. Amid conflict, these differing perspectives caused dismay and disagreement among members about how leadership decisions were reached and communicated.

Perhaps one of the most interesting questions for intersectional congregations focuses on pastoral leadership. While these churches define themselves by their desire to be diverse, they are, in the majority, led by pastors who are white, male, cisgender, and straight. This probably reflects the generational reality that, while female pastors are increasingly in the vanguard of leadership of all kinds of mainline Protestant denominational churches, most churches today are led by straight, white, male pastors. As this has changed—and will continue to change—intersectional churches face the proverbial "opportunities and challenges" that come with transition and leadership, as well as learning to follow leaders of differing perspectives and identities.

LEADERSHIP IN INNOVATION, AGILITY, AND PEACEMAKING

By necessity born out of their histories and circumstances, by the courage of their pastors and membership, and through the inherent openness of their congregations, these churches model innovation, adaptability, and a comfort with risk-taking. These examples may encourage other mainline Protestant congregations to follow suit. These congregations' DNA of comfort with experimentation teaches them lessons born of success and failure, conflict and peacemaking. They view membership and participation of friends of the church more informally and openly. They practice governance in ways that seek to correct the historical failures of white heterosupremacy. Several, for example, place great emphasis on leadership development, identifying members representing a cross section of diversity with an emphasis on those who otherwise might not emerge or self-nominate for leadership and equipping them to lead with skills their backgrounds or jobs may not have fostered.

These congregations work beyond their walls to make peace through external advocacy, mission, and outreach. They also find the power and priority of relationships helps them get through times of disagreement. That speaks loudly to deeply divided denominations in a deeply divided country. They point to Christ's command to seek unity amid diversity, which can happen, as one pastor summarily notes, when members in disagreement simply practice respect for diversity.

A NEW HOPE, A PARTICULAR PRECARIOUSNESS

These intersectional congregations bear witness to new ministry and faith expression rarely replicated in more established churches. (I should note—and celebrate—that the New Worshipping Communities initiative of the PC(USA) and similar "research and development" arms of other mainline denominations are launching a range of new congregations and faith expressions with intersectional leadership and diversity primarily in mind.)

Among the more established congregations I learned about, their new life reflects a particular authenticity, organic and unpredictable. It's a mission refined from hard lessons learned from intersecting an array of members' experiences, perspectives, opinions, wounds, and healing.

The work and ministry of these churches reflect the commitment to live out of their multilayered diversity openly, knowing this road brings bumps and sharp curves. Each in their own way, as instructed by their constitution, seek to model "a new openness" in membership, "becoming in fact, as well as in faith, a community of women and men of all ages, races, ethnicities, and worldly conditions, made one in Christ by the power of the Spirit, as a visible sign of the new humanity;" as well as a "more radical obedience to Christ, and to a more joyous celebration in worship and work."[2]

But these congregations also live on the edge. Most mainline Protestant churches today face existential questions that will come to a head sooner or later. The economic and institutional fallout from the COVID-19 pandemic risks accelerating the end for many struggling churches. One way or another, thousands will close in the next two decades as the church's failure to reach younger generations plays out.

While intersectional churches know the gifts of dynamic and ever-deepening life together, they exist with unique precariousness within these broader headwinds facing the church at large. As noted by their pastors, with respect to mission, several of these churches acknowledged the dangers. In the words of one pastor, these congregations can risk being "all over the place" in missions and outreach. These intersectional churches are, by nature, challenged to represent a wide range of interests and expressions. However, most often, they live with notable limitations in financial resources and leadership. Many supplement their budgets by renting space because tithes and offerings fall short of their expenses. Several are blessed with endowments, but they are also burdened with large, beautiful but aging sanctuaries and other buildings and grounds responsibilities.

Their fragility—and new possibility—goes beyond financial resources. In terms of their "human capital," these congregations focus internally on leadership development that must account for varying learning styles, educational backgrounds, levels of familiarity with polity, and different denominational backgrounds.

Finally, an objective outlook for these churches must acknowledge their futures are as challenged as America's itself. As with the country, these congregations ride the waves of diversity across race, gender, sexual orientation, class, and other factors of diversity. While they can shine a light for the future of the country, they face the same open-ended questions about how or whether America will achieve a more peaceful and harmonious accord, particularly along lines of race, and how America will deal with the cancer of white supremacy.

The PC(USA) is like most mainline Protestant congregations. Despite concerted efforts and the expense of millions of dollars toward denominational programming over the decades, it remains stubbornly segregated and 90 percent white. Meanwhile, the nation moves relentlessly toward its twofold future of rapid urbanization and a "majority-minority" population. These urban churches point the way to a more diverse body of Christ. But as more and more young people leave the church at large, the question remains as to whether these congregations will see more success—or less—in engaging younger generations that have lost faith and confidence in the church.

Perhaps, in his own way and in his own time, the apostle Paul knew similar questions as he wrote to the beginning disciples at Colossae, echoing his advice to the Galatians about how we can bring and preserve our respective identities into a community renewed in Christ:

> In that renewal there is no longer Greek and Jew, circumcised and uncircumcised, barbarian, Scythian, slave and free; but Christ is all and in all! As God's chosen ones, holy and beloved, clothe yourselves with compassion, kindness, humility, meekness, and patience. Bear with one another and, if anyone has a complaint against another, forgive each other; just as the Lord has forgiven you, so you also must forgive. Above all, clothe yourselves with love, which binds everything together in perfect harmony. And let the peace of Christ rule in your hearts, to which indeed

you were called in the one body. And be thankful. Let the word of Christ dwell in you richly; teach and admonish one another in all wisdom; and with gratitude in your hearts sing psalms, hymns, and spiritual songs to God. And whatever you do, in word or deed, do everything in the name of the Lord Jesus, giving thanks to God the Father through him.[3]

TRANSFORMATION

Active membership in any church will eventually bring its questions, complications, and disappointments, if not its bumps, bruises, and scars. If taken seriously, the gospel itself comes into conflict with the culture, and Christ left us, you and me—flawed, bumbling, and broken human beings—in charge of the church. If there is to be an intersectional church, potential members should know it isn't for the casually involved Christian. Nor is it for families who bring a consumer mindset to church, expecting it to meet their individual needs, demands, and busy schedules without an equal commitment to bearing witness to those beyond the church campus in the form of justice and mercy.

But the promise of the church is the transformation of its disciples as they experience healing, embrace, redemption, and a renewed sense of call. Powerful stories of learning and growth emerge from these journeys, stories of what God is up to in these places.

You met Johnny Johnson in the opening chapter, a banker and Caldwell member who shares this story:

I was born in the church and [was] always taken to church on Sunday mornings. That continued into my adult life. Church was just what you did on Sunday.

I eventually came to terms that I was a gay man and I wanted to embrace that. But the church was not embracing that. There was no sermon I ever heard on tolerance toward gay people like me. This was back in the 1980s and people were dying left and right of AIDS, and the church was silent.

I got very angry and I left the church. I didn't leave God. I still prayed occasionally, but I did not come to church. I did not support the church. Years later, a friend invited me to a church and I came kicking and screaming. Then I cried for the entire hour. This church is black and white, gay and straight, rich and poor, and I think my identity is a real asset. I am free to be me.

Another kind of transformation that happens at intersectional churches is that of cisgender white folk who yearn to see a different world, one free of prejudice and bitter division, one in which we live out of deeper understanding and empathy and are freed from our blindness to be one in Christ. Caldwell member Linda Horton once described her transformation this way:

> I thought I was pretty open about other people's beliefs and other people's faiths. But I really had a lot of work to do and I still have a lot of work to do. But this particular church has taken me so far on my journey that I really can't put it into words.
>
> I keep remembering a quote from [former civil rights leader, Atlanta mayor and US ambassador to the United Nations] Andrew Young. He was marching with Dr. King in Selma and he and his wife lived in the country outside of Selma, which is really close to where I was raised. There were some people who wanted to

come talk to him, [but] not about good things. They wanted to threaten him and try to run him out of town. He was trying to get his wife to sit in the front window of their house with a shotgun, just in case he needed backup. She turned to him and said, "If you can't lift those white hoods and see the people under them as children of God just like you are, then you don't need to say you are a Christian."

I think we are trying to lift everybody's hoods and see everyone as a child of God.

10

LIBERATION ...
IN CHRIST

If you have come to help me, you are wasting your time.
But if you have come because your liberation is bound
up with mine, then let us work together.

—Lilla Watson, *Aboriginal elder,*
educator, and activist

A Caldwell member tells a story about her past adventures
as a weekend pilot. In one of her first solo flights, she lost
track of her exact surroundings in the air over Greenville,
South Carolina. She looked out the window and spotted an
airfield. Knowing they could help, she got on the radio and
confessed her confusion.

"This is 4326 Delta Charlie. I am temporarily disoriented
somewhere over Greenville and requesting assistance."

She then learned the airfield below was a military base.
But, thankfully, rather than shooting her down or scram-
bling the jets to chase her away, the base tower calmly
guided her to another nearby airfield where she made a safe
landing with a great tale to tell.

I shared that story on the Sunday following the 2016 president election, a weak attempt on my part, perhaps, to lighten the weight we all felt after the shock and dismay of Donald Trump's victory. On that November Sunday, along with most of the nation, we were just beginning to sort out what has become painfully clear since—how almost half of our nation actually felt about the sweeping demographic changes afoot and who they were willing to trust to try to change the nation's course.

As with our pilot, the 2016 presidential election left many feeling awfully disoriented. The years since have proved that feeling to be anything but temporary. For the church, two truths loom. First, despite how so many fear-driven voters feel, the future of demographic and cultural change in America is cast. America will be a majority-minority nation. Second, the nation seems likely to continue to lose faith in organized religion, at least in how the church at large has expressed itself for centuries. As these dual realities come to fruition over the next one or two generations, we are in for a time of slow and desperate resistance to these changes and an ongoing effort by some to return to "the good old days." But those days are not coming back.

Where will the church stand amid this crisis of conscience? Will the church become a sanctuary for all? Will the church be an agent of hope and a helpful midwife as our nation goes through the labor pains of becoming something new?

I happened to be preaching through Galatians in the autumn 2016 when America's deep divisions came into a new clarity of focus. Paul's words to the divided in Galatia spoke then and they continue to speak to us today. But God's people have seen division many times before. In first-century Galatia, the powerful traditionalists sought to hold sway over newcomers to Christ, insisting on a litmus test of faith, namely circumcision, even as Christ had erased the need for such things.

In much of America today, defenders of the status quo are doing the same, denying Christ's invitation to find unity amid diversity, oneness in God's peace and justice. In Galatia, the traditionalists feared change, namely that Christ had changed everything and that the powerful few no longer held the keys to access God. Their strategy was to divide the Jesus movement and intimidate the powerless back into submission. In America today, a similar fear and desperate grasp for power and privilege are the demon that possesses too much of God's church and too many of God's people.

Paul saw something new was needed. Having stepped away from his own power and privilege, Paul took the side of the oppressed, as our "othered" theologians point out in their commentaries on Galatians. How many of God's people will take the same step and begin the same journey?

As we hear the call to work across our differences and benefit from new perspectives, some may accept that invitation. Many won't. But wherever we may find ourselves in this debate, Paul's words shine a light. The church is called to resist judgment of the other as well as the false hope that radical individualism and self-sufficiency offers, at least to some. Instead, the church is called to invest itself, as it always has, in community and the common good in a newly pluralistic America. Relative to our past plodding, that investment must be done in increasingly bold ways.

The road to peace is outlined by justice, mercy, compassion, and love as taught by Christ and in the undeserved grace his death obtained for all. On that road and in its intersections, as Paul wrote, we can learn to "bear one another's burdens" and deepen our wells of empathy in a compassion-starved time.

To follow that road, many of us first need liberation from whatever keeps us stationary and shackled to a past that won't come again. Our liberator, as Paul wrote to the Galatians, is Christ. In Christ, God flattened the mountains and filled the valleys that separate us across all of our self-imposed lines of division and separation. In Christ's call to unity amid diversity, we are freed from the myopia of just one perspective or experience, namely ours and those like us. In Christ, God invites us to become one even while we are many by putting one identity over all others, that of love.

As many of you as were baptized into Christ have clothed yourselves with Christ. There is no longer Jew or Greek, there is no longer slave or free, there is no longer male and female; for all of you are one in Christ.[1]

For the future of the mainline Protestant church to be a just, inclusive, welcoming, and renewing community, God in Christ invites us to honor each experience as something that builds up the whole rather than something that tears down our individual walled-off existence, identity, and "truth." God calls us to follow faith, not fear. Christ came to help us see and build a new thing.

It is a road where labels like gay, straight, trans, cisgender, queer, Black, brown, white, rich, poor, suburban, urban, rural, Democrat, Republican, or Independent should no longer serve as concrete lane dividers. It is a place where fear and hate no longer fuel white nationalism and global isolationist thinking. It is a place of all perspectives and experiences, where the wounded and hurting are embraced alongside the healthy and the strong. It is a place where, as

Paul wrote to the Galatians, "the only thing that counts is faith working through love."

Through seasons of difficulty and joy, failure and success, these congregations have learned how to love each other come what may. They have loved their way even while getting bruised in the process. They have emerged stronger and more alive. These churches have learned the truth of our baptism belief that to live fully in Christ we must first die to ourselves.

In an essay about Rev. Dr. Martin Luther King Jr., my father, a civil rights journalist, wrote about Dr. King as liberator, preaching freedom for some of us from hate, prejudice, and blinding privilege; freedom from the toxic, soul-crushing effect of being the oppressor. He called Rev. Dr. King "the Black Emancipator of enslaved Southern white folk" with "his capacity to combine passion for justice with a loving cunning that made some people call him soft."[2]

Too many of us are still enslaved by the fear of change and our perception that we will lose more than we gain as our nation and our churches change in the years to come. We are captive, kept from the freedom that is God's gift to us in Christ, who insists there can be unity in diversity. It's not easy to die to ourselves that we may live as one in Christ. Still, Christ's liberating grace reaches back for us and for the mainline Protestant church. It offers to place us at the intersection where our future lies, where we can be liberated from the tyranny of our own oppression, a place where God is waiting.

As one who is still on a journey of liberation, I am far, far from anything close to perfect freedom or clarity. Yet, I can attest to a wondrous emancipation I could never have imagined for myself and others at Caldwell Presbyterian. The same goes for the congregations that shared their stories for this work as they live though the radical hospitality, glorious messiness, and constructive tension that is the intersectional church.

Each of us has been offered freedom, as Paul wrote to the Galatians, to "stand firm" and not "submit again to the yoke of slavery" of our position and privilege, our history or heritage, or whatever limits others may try to place on our identity. The gift for people who look like me is emancipation itself.

And, as I have glimpsed at Caldwell, it is not just for people who look like me or share my personal journey. It is the opportunity for the gay, white, professional man to walk with the Black, Muslim friend of Caldwell who spent forty years in prison, has reentered society, and is constantly "loving neighbor." It is the chance for the straight, Black woman who struggles in poverty to find commonality in Christ with her white, lesbian sister as she grieves the loss of her partner of thirty years. It is for white parents to listen as Black parents explain how they must have "the talk" with their children in case they get pulled over by police.

It is for all to listen to the truth of our interracial couples as they, still, encounter rooms full of hostile stares anytime they are out. It is for our young adults to walk with our older members and discover both the pain of ageism and the wonder of aging gracefully and courageously. It is for those with mental illnesses to be able to speak openly about their struggles with anxiety, depression, bipolar disorder, addiction, and other "invisible" conditions. It is for all of us to understand what it is to live with HIV. It is for those with meager resources to understand through the testimony and experiences of their more affluent pew mates that money is not the answer to all problems.

Is the mainline Protestant church prepared to die to itself in at least some ways? Die to its usual ways and its usual structures, its timidity and its pragmatic, management-approach to ministry? Die to the latent homophobia, sexism, and racism that still shape its ways, perhaps more than it realizes? Die to its inflexibility and unwillingness to worship in new and different ways informed by other cultures and traditions? Die to its tendency to follow dogma and doctrine over the living witness of Christ Jesus? Die to its all-consuming fear that in its current forms, it just might plain-old die?

What do we follow? Whom do we trust? Where do we look for liberation if not in the God who defeated death for all time and calls us to live in response, even in ways we may think are reckless? What holds us prisoner? What shackles us to being a church that is about 90 percent white when our cities and, soon enough, our nation look nothing like that? What life are we losing as we try to outsmart or outspend the trends of declining membership, confidence, and faith in the church?

The God of our emancipation is not finished.

God's church will not die.

With that promise of God's unmerited grace through Christ in our hearts, will we give ourselves to its ongoing rebirth and renewal for a new day?

EPILOGUE

The year 2020 began hopefully enough. Then, as the season of Lent led to Easter, our national life seemed to slow down and accelerate at once.

COVID-19 drove Americans home and the economy into lower gear. Unprecedented in a century, the virus forced us to renegotiate every aspect of our lives, including our ministries at Caldwell.

Then Ahmaud Arbery. Then Breonna Taylor. Then George Floyd, whose killing by the Minneapolis police, captured so vividly and awfully on a cell phone video, stirred something deep in the heart of America.

In cities and towns from coast to coast, hundreds of thousands of people of all kinds demonstrated nightly for weeks. In Charlotte, I once again found myself in my stole on the streets and the interstates as a peacekeeper and witness to the palpable pain of my friends of color. Charlotte police gassed Caldwell's youth minister, Rev. Justin Martin, while he was peacefully protesting, one of two strategic mistakes that led to more than one hundred clergy in Charlotte calling for police reform.

Driven by dramatic shifts in white peoples' responses, public opinion polls pointed to what seemed to be a tipping point in the national consciousness in regard to racial injustice. Books about racism and how to combat it shot up the best-seller lists. Intersectional thinking advanced as many

LGBTQ and feminist organizations raised their voices to say "Black Lives Matter" more loudly and deliberately than ever before.

As George Floyd's last breath breathed life anew into the nation's struggle against racial injustice, white folks seemed changed. Many Black folks thought to themselves, "We'll see" and "Let us pray."

It was time for Caldwell Presbyterian to pray, too, but not just that. The congregation had digested, studied, and faithfully pondered the truth about how the Caldwell fortune, left to the church a century before, had been made on a plantation north of Charlotte. My sermon on June 27, 2020, included these thoughts:

> For the past few weeks, I have had something laying heavy on my heart and mind. As America seems to be trying to become something new, the country is putting away the monuments to the confederacy and its champions that have long been a thorn deep in the side of our Black siblings.
>
> That conversation does not exclude us at the corner of Park and Fifth. It was there, at the height of Jim Crow days, when whites were doing all they could to rewrite history, intimidate Blacks, and save the "lost cause," that a fortune fell here, into the laps of the members of what was then called John Knox Presbyterian Church....
>
> [They] received that fortune and renamed their church Caldwell Memorial Presbyterian. A church named to memorialize those who owned and enslaved other human beings, beloved dark-skinned children of God kidnapped from their homeland and forced to spill their blood, sweat, tears, and lives to make a fortune for the Caldwell family.

Many of us have known this complicated, tortuous truth for six or seven years now. We have been disturbed by it and lived uncomfortably with it. We have not finished determining what to do about it.

I believe that time is now. As a church that strives toward being antiracist, as a church that seeks to follow God's invitation by welcoming all, as a church that will literally become home to people of color in the next two years, as a church that God saved from extinction to do extraordinary things . . . it is time, perhaps it is past time, for truth and reconciliation. Truth, full truth, about what our name stands for, and reconciliation with whether we should hold on to it. Either way, I am sure God can bless us in this conversation.

Days later, the session laid out a process for listening to the congregation for an answer to those questions. By the time you read this, our church may have a new name, and I have no idea what it may be. An interesting twist is that the first "Caldwell Presbyterian" in the area was a church for freed Blacks from the Caldwell plantation started by Northern Presbyterians just after the Civil War. So, the name "Caldwell" could stand for the enslavers or the enslaved. Or the congregation may go in a new direction. Whatever the name is, I pray it honors the Lord and gives hope to the hopeless.

In his master work, *How to Be an Antiracist*, Ibram X. Kendi describes racism as "one of the fastest-spreading and most fatal cancers humanity has ever known."[1] At the corner of Park and Fifth Streets in Charlotte, North Carolina, we have so much to learn and experience about how to add our few ounces of chemotherapy to the fight. As I learned from watching my mother battle leukemia for fifteen years, chemo tends to make you feel worse before you feel better. That may be true with us and with America.

What I love about the odd but brave flock my colleagues and I are blessed to pastor is its faithful courage. Its crazy dream to build twenty-one apartments, which admittedly may be the widow's mite against our city's 35,000-unit affordable housing shortage. Its striving to welcome and understand all of those along the entire LGBTQ spectrum. Its commitment to reversing the pain the church at large has visited upon the othered and the marginalized. Its calling to liberate white folks from the imprisonment of their privilege. Its hunger to seek God's will and Christ's heart, whatever the risk. Its faith that God is continually moving us all along John Newton's own pathway of "I once was lost but now am found, was blind, but now I see."

In the end, what sticks with me are the words my mother prayed nightly at the dinner table, from 1 Corinthians 13:12:

> For now we see in a mirror, dimly, but then we will see face to face. Now I know only in part; then I will know fully, even as I have been fully known.

Notes

Introduction

1. This book will also use the abbreviation PC(USA) when referring to Presbyterian Church (USA).
2. Gal 3:27–28.

Chapter 1: The First Church of the Island of Misfit Toys

1. For example, see Patricia Hill Collins and Sirma Bilge, *Intersectionality* (Cambridge, UK: Polity Press, 2016) or Grace Ji-Sun Kim and Susan Shaw, eds., *Intersectional Theology: An Introductory Guide* (Minneapolis: Fortress Press, 2018).
2. "Kimberlé Crenshaw on Intersectionality, More Than Two Decades Later," Columbia Law School, posted June 8, 2017, https://tinyurl.com/yy9m86 n4.

Chapter 3: Is Anyone out There?

1. Stef W. Kight, "America's Majority Minority Future," Axios, April 29, 2019, https://tinyurl.com /yyut7dq7.
2. Kight, "America's Majority Minority Future."

3. Nate Berg, "US Metros Are Ground Zero for Majority-Minority Populations," CityLab, May 18, 2012, https://tinyurl.com/ybazkz2h.

4. Kight, "America's Majority Minority Future."

5. Grace Ji-Sun Kim and Susan Shaw, *Intersectional Theology: An Introductory Guide* (Minneapolis: Fortress Press, 2018). In this paragraph, they pull heavily from Daniel Cox and Robert P. Jones, *America's Changing Religious Identity* (Washington, DC: PRRI, September 6, 2017), https://tiny url.com/yd5lnt6e.

6. Pew Research Center, "Attitudes on Same-Sex Marriage," May 14, 2019, https://tinyurl.com /ybowh8y3.

7. Office of the General Assembly Presbyterian Church, Book of Order (Louisville: Presbyterian Publishing Corporation, 2019), 6.

8. LifeWay, "Research: Racial Diversity at Church More Dream Than Reality," January 17, 2014, https://tinyurl.com/y6wbcg6d.

9. Assata Zerai, *Intersectionality in Intentional Communities: The Struggle for Inclusivity in Multicultural US Protestant Congregations* (Lanham, MD: Lexington Books, 2016), 135.

10. "Our History and Who We Are," Brown Memorial Park Avenue Presbyterian, accessed May 5, 2020, https://tinyurl.com/y8h5tpnl.

11. Brown Memorial, "Our History."

12. Andrew Michaels, "Founders Remember Oaklands Presbyterian over Five Decades," May 12, 2016, https://tinyurl.com/y7lzjg69.

13. Zerai, *Intersectionality in Intentional Communities*, 69.

CHAPTER 4: THE CHURCH OF BOTH/AND

1. Patricia Hill Collins and Sirma Bilge, *Intersectionality* (Cambridge, UK: Polity Press, 2016).
2. Lisa M. Krieger, "Women's March Brought Millions to the Streets, but Figuring Out How Many Is an Imperfect Science," *San Jose Mercury News*, updated January 24, 2017, https://tinyurl.com/ybgp8sjl.
3. Rebecca Klar, "Poll: Patriotism, Religion, Kids, Lower Priorities for Younger Americans," The Hill, August 25, 2019, https://tinyurl.com/ybgv5peq.
4. Zerai, *Intersectionality in Intentional Communities*, 2.
5. Zerai, *Intersectionality in Intentional Communities*, 11.
6. Grace Ji-Sun Kim and Susan Shaw, eds., *Intersectional Theology: An Introductory Guide* (Minneapolis: Fortress Press, 2018), xv.
7. Kim and Shaw, *Intersectional Theology*, 53.
8. Hab 2:9, NIV.
9. Kim and Shaw, *Intersectional Theology*, 58.
10. Kim and Shaw, *Intersectional Theology*, 68.
11. Kim and Shaw, *Intersectional Theology*, 95.

CHAPTER 5: CENTERING "OTHERED" VIEWS OF SCRIPTURE

1. Gal 2:16.
2. Gal 5:4; Peterson, *The Message*.
3. Gal 3:27–28, NRSV.
4. Brad R. Braxton, *No Longer Slaves: Galatians and African American Experience* (Collegeville, MN: Liturgical Press, 2002), 78.

5. Braxton, *No Longer Slaves*, 93.

6. Braxton, *No Longer Slaves*, 95.

7. Braxton, *No Longer Slaves*, 95.

8. Brian K. Blount, quoted in Brad R. Braxton, "Galatians," in *True to Our Native Land: An African American New Testament Commentary*, ed. Brian K. Blount, Cain Hope Felder, Clarice J. Martin, and Emerson B. Powery (Minneapolis: Fortress Press, 2007), 343.

9. Brigitte Kahl, "Galatians: On Discomfort about Gender and Other Problems of Otherness," in *Feminist Biblical Interpretation: A Compendium of Critical Commentary on the Books of the Bible and Related Literature*, ed. Luise Schottroff and Marie-Theres Wacker (Grand Rapids, MI: Eerdmans, 2012), 755–66.

10. Kahl, "Galatians," 755.

11. Kahl, "Galatians," 755.

12. Kahl, "Galatians," 757.

13. Kahl, "Galatians," 758.

14. Kahl, "Galatians," 759.

15. Raquel St. Clair, "Womanist Biblical Interpretation," in *True to Our Native Land: An African American New Testament Commentary*, ed. Brian K. Blount, Cain Hope Felder, Clarice J. Martin, and Emerson B. Powery (Minneapolis: Fortress Press, 2007), 54.

16. St. Clair, "Womanist," 57.

17. St. Clair, "Womanist," 55.

18. Patrick S. Cheng, *Radical Love: An Introduction to Queer Theology* (New York: Seabury Books, 2011), 9.

19. Cheng, *Radical Love*, 45.

20. Cheng, *Radical Love*, 94.

21. Cheng, *Radical Love*, 100.
22. Cheng, *Radical Love*, 626.
23. Cheng, *Radical Love*, 627.
24. Cheng, *Radical Love*, 629.
25. Horace L. Griffin, *Their Own Receive Them Not: African American Lesbians and Gays in Black Churches* (Eugene, OR: Wipf and Stock, 2010), 95–96.
26. Griffin, *Their Own*, 101.
27. Griffin, *Their Own*, 140.
28. Griffin, *Their Own*, 192.
29. Griffin, *Their Own*, 193.
30. Griffin, *Their Own*, 199.
31. Griffin, *Their Own*, 205.
32. Griffin, *Their Own*, 222.
33. Griffin, *Their Own*, 223.
34. Gal 3:27–28.

CHAPTER 6: THE CHURCH OF BOTH/AND: JUSTICE AND . . . (EVERYTHING)

1. Amos 5:21–24.
2. *The Presbyterian Outlook*, August 19, 2019.
3. Emmanuel Y. Lartey, *In Living Color: An Intercultural Approach to Pastoral Care and Counseling* (London: Jessica Kingsley Publishers, 2003), 55–59.
4. Lartey, *In Living Color*, 171.
5. Sheryl A. Kujawa-Holbrook and Karen B. Montagno, eds., *Injustice and the Care of Souls: Taking Oppression Seriously in Pastoral Care* (Minneapolis: Fortress Press, 2009), 16.
6. Kujawa-Holbrook and Montagno, *Injustice*, 18.

7. Rachel Pacheco, email message to author, November 2016.
8. Nibs Stroupe and Caroline Leach, O Lord, Hold Our Hands: How a Church Thrives in a Multicultural World (Louisville: William John Knox, 2003), 20.
9. Adriene Thorne, email message to author, November 2016.
10. Annual Church Statistical Report, PC(USA) Research Office data for 2018.

CHAPTER 7: THE BOTH/AND OF REPAIR AND RECONCILIATION

1. Jennifer Harvey, Dear White Christians: For Those Still Longing for Racial Reconciliation (Grand Rapids, MI: Eerdmans, 2014), 2.
2. Harvey, White Christians, 5.
3. Harvey, White Christians, 5.
4. Harvey, White Christians, 163.
5. Harvey, White Christians, 159.
6. Harvey, White Christians, 167.
7. Harvey, White Christians, 170.
8. Jeanna Wortham, "A 'Glorious Poetic Rage,'" New York Times, June 8, 2020, https://tinyurl.com/yde8ypel.

CHAPTER 8: POSSIBILITIES AND POTENTIAL PITFALLS

1. Brad Christerson and Michael Emerson, "The Costs of Diversity in Religious Organizations: An In-Depth Case Study," Sociology of Religion 64, no.

2 (Summer 2003): 167, https://doi.org/10.2307/3712369.

2. Christerson and Emerson, "Costs of Diversity," 167.
3. Acts 4:32.
4. Gal 6:2.
5. Lartey, *In Living Color*, 153. Emphasis original.
6. Kujawa-Holbrook and Montagno, *Injustice*, 16.
7. 2 Cor 11:30.

CHAPTER 9: LESSONS LEARNED

1. "Carol of the Epiphany," by John Bell (Mt.2:1-2). © 1992 WGRG the Iona Community (Scotland) admin. by GIA Publications, Inc. Used by permission.
2. Presbyterian Church, Book of Order, 6.
3. Col 3:11–17.

CHAPTER 10: LIBERATION . . . IN CHRIST

1. Gal 3:27–28.
2. Reese Cleghorn, "My Grandfather and the Cyclone," in *You Can't Eat Magnolias*, ed. Brandt Ayers and Thomas Naylor (Oxford, MS: The L.Q.C. Lamar Society, 1972), 35.

EPILOGUE

1. Ibram X. Kendi, *How to Be an Antiracist* (New York: One World, 2020), 238.

BIBLIOGRAPHY

Blount, Brian, and Lenora Tubbs Tisdale, eds. *Making Room at the Table: An Invitation to Multicultural Worship*. Louisville: Westminster John Knox Press, 2001.

Blount, Brian, ed. *True to Our Native Land*. Minneapolis: Fortress Press, 2007.

Bowers, Laurene Beth. *Becoming a Multicultural Church*. Cleveland: The Pilgrim Press, 2006.

Braxton, Brad R. *No Longer Slaves: Galatians and the African American Experience*. Collegeville, MN: The Liturgical Press, 2002.

Cheng, Patrick S. "Galatians." In *The Queer Bible Commentary*, edited by Robert Goss and Mona West. London: SCM Press, 2006.

———. *Radical Love: An Introduction to Queer Theology*. New York: Seabury Books, 2011.

Christerson, Brad, and Michael Emerson. "The Costs of Diversity in Religious Organizations: An In-Depth Case Study." *Sociology of Religion* 64, no. 2. (Summer 2003): 163–81. https://doi.org/10.2307/3712369.

Cohn, D'Vera, and Andrea Caumont. "10 Demographic Trends Shaping the US and the World in 2016." Pew Research Center, March 31, 2016. https://archive.is/zWfEW.

Collins, Patricia Hill, and Sirma Bilge. *Intersectionality*. Cambridge, UK: Polity Press, 2016.

Duncan, Lenny. *Dear Church: A Love Letter from a Black Preacher to the Whitest Denomination in the US.* Minneapolis: Fortress Press, 2019.

Griffin, Horace L. *Their Own Receive Them Not.* Eugene, OR: Wipf and Stock, 2010.

Hankivsky, Olena. *Intersectionality 101.* Vancouver, BC: Institute for Intersectionality Research and Policy at Simon Fraser University, 2014. https://tinyurl.com/y84kzf6p.

Harvey, Jennifer. *Dear White Christians: For Those Still Longing for Racial Reconciliation.* Grand Rapids, MI: Eerdmans, 2014.

Jennings, Willie James. *The Christian Imagination: Theology and the Origins of Race.* New Haven, CT: Yale University Press, 2010.

Kahl, Brigitte. "Galatians: On Discomfort About Gender and Other Problems of Otherness." In *Feminist Biblical Interpretation: A Compendium of Critical Commentary on the Books of the Bible and Related Literature,* edited by Louise Schottroff, Marie-Theres Wacker, and Martin Rumscheidt. Grand Rapids, MI: Eerdmans, 2012.

Kim, Grace Ji-Sun, and Susan Shaw. *Intersectional Theology: An Introductory Guide.* Minneapolis: Fortress Press, 2018.

Krieger, Lisa M. "Women's March Brought Millions to the Streets, but Figuring Out How Many Is an Imperfect Science." *San Jose Mercury News,* updated January 24, 2017. https://archive.is/6cWib.

Kujwa-Holbrook, Sheryl A., and Karen B. Montagno, eds. *Injustice and the Care of Souls.* Minneapolis: Fortress Press, 2009.

Lartey, Emmanuel Y. *In Living Color: An Intercultural Approach to Pastoral Care and Counseling.* London: Jessica Kingsley Publishers, 2003.

Lewis, Jacqueline, and John Janka. *The Pentecost Paradigm: Ten Strategies for Becoming a Multiracial Congregation.* Louisville: William John Knox Press, 2018.

Office of the General Assembly Presbyterian Church. Book of Order. Louisville: Presbyterian Publishing Corporation, 2019.

Oswald, Roy M. "How to Minister Effectively in Family, Pastoral, Program, and Corporate Sized Churches." *Action Information* XVII, no. 2, (1991); Volume XVII, Number 3, 1991.

Pew Research Center. "Attitudes on Same-Sex Marriage." Last modified May 14, 2019. https://tinyurl.com/ybowh8y3.

Richardson, Ronald. *Creating a Healthier Church: Family Systems Theory, Leadership, and Congregational Life.* Minneapolis: Fortress Press, 1996.

Sanders, Cody J., and Angela Yarber. *Microaggressions in Ministry: Confronting the Hidden Violence in Everyday Church.* Louisville: Westminster John Knox Press, 2015.

St. Clair, Raquel. "Womanist Biblical Interpretation." In *True to Our Native Land,* edited by Brian Blount, Cain Hope Felder, Clarice J. Martin, ad Emerson B. Powery. Minneapolis: Fortress Press, 2007.

Stroupe, Nibs, and Caroline Leach. *O Lord, Hold Our Hands: How a Church Thrives in a Multicultural World.* Louisville: Westminster John Knox Press, 2003.

Zerai, Assata. *Intersectionality in Intentional Communities: The Struggle for Inclusivity in Multicultural US Protestant Congregations.* Lanham, MD: Lexington Books, 2016.